God Only Knows

God Only Knows

Faith, Hope, Love,
and
The Beach Boys

Edited by
JEFF SELLARS

CASCADE *Books* • Eugene, Oregon

GOD ONLY KNOWS
Faith, Hope, Love, and The Beach Boys

Copyright © 2015 Wipf and Stock Publishers. All rights reserved. Except for brief quotations in critical publications or reviews, no part of this book may be reproduced in any manner without prior written permission from the publisher. Write: Permissions, Wipf and Stock Publishers, 199 W. 8th Ave., Suite 3, Eugene, OR 97401.

Cascade Books
An Imprint of Wipf and Stock Publishers
199 W. 8th Ave., Suite 3
Eugene, OR 97401

www.wipfandstock.com

ISBN 13: 978-1-4982-0766-9

Cataloguing-in-Publication Data

God only knows : faith, hope, love, and the Beach Boys / edited by Jeff Sellars.

xii + 168 p. ; 23 cm. Includes bibliographical references and indices.

ISBN 13: 978-1-4982-0766-9

1. Beach Boys. 2. Brian Wilson, 1942–. 3. Theology. 4. Philosophy. I. Sellars, Jeff. II. Title.

ML420.W5525 G35 2015

Manufactured in the U.S.A.   12/14/2015

Contents

Acknowledgments | vii
Notes on Contributors | ix

Introduction | 1
   —Jeff Sellars

One
Wonderful Thing: A Children's Song! Brian Wilson, *SMiLE*, and Faith | 9
   —Steven R. Guthrie

Two
Emersonian Individualism and the Quest for Wholeness in *Pet Sounds* | 27
   —Thomas M. Kitts

Three
Dire Wave: Brian Wilson's "'Til I Die" | 47
   —Dave Perkins

Four
Searching for the Perfect Wave: The Beach Boys and the Power of Hope | 67
   —Mary McDonough

Five
Surf's Up: A Spirituality of Awakening and Hope in the Beach Boys | 82
   —William Walker

Six
You Need a Mess of Help to Stand Alone: Vulnerability, Judgment, and Love in the Music and Life of Brian Wilson | 95
   —David Zahl

Seven
"I See Love": Perceiving and Building Up Love in *Sunflower* | 110
   —Jeff Sellars

Eight
Apocalypse of Love: The Event of *Pet Sounds* in Process Perspective | 126
 —Austin J. Roberts

Bibliography | 143
Index | 151

Acknowledgments

I (Jeff Sellars) would like to thank all of the contributors in this volume for their work, help, and patience. I would especially like to single out Thomas Kitts and Mary McDonough for their counsel during the process of putting this project together—and Austin Roberts for his extra help in getting this project off the ground. Another special thanks must also go to Kevin C. Neece, who helped in gathering prospective contributors and assisted in the shaping of this project.

Notes on Contributors

Steven Guthrie joined the Belmont School of Religion in August of 2005, after teaching for five years at the University of St. Andrews in St. Andrews, Scotland. During his time in Scotland, Dr. Guthrie was on the faculty of the Institute for Theology, Imagination and the Arts, and he came to Belmont to help launch a new program in Religion and the Arts. Dr. Guthrie earned an undergraduate degree in music theory from the University of Michigan, and worked for several years as a musician before becoming disoriented on the way to a gig and stumbling into the world of academic theology. In his spare time, he enjoys playing his Fender Rhodes, eating pizza, or simply quietly meditating on the goodness of the Pittsburgh Steelers. Above all, he enjoys writing breezy, faintly humorous autobiographical paragraphs for the Internet; always written in the third person, so that the casual reader will believe that they have been penned by some devoted chronicler of his life and work. Dr. Guthrie is married to Julie and has four extraordinarily clever and impossibly good-looking children. On weekends you will regularly find him gigging with the band SixtyFour. He is the author of *Creator Spirit: The Holy Spirit and the Art of Becoming Human*, Baker Academic, 2011, and the editor (with Dr. Jeremy Begbie) of *Resonant Witness: Conversations between Music and Theology*.

Thomas M. Kitts, PhD, Professor of English at St. John's University, New York, is the author of *John Fogerty: American Son*; *Ray Davies: Not Like Everybody Else*; and *The Theatrical Life of George Henry Boker*. He has edited the essay collections *Finding Fogerty: Interdisciplinary Readings of John Fogerty and CCR*; *Crossing Aesthetic Borders with the Kinks*; and the anthology *Literature and Work*. With Gary Burns of Northern Illinois University, he edits *Popular Music and Society* and *Rock Music Studies*.

Notes on Contributors

Mary McDonough, JD, PhD, is a 2015–2016 Research Fellow through Harvard University's Department of Global Health and Social Medicine. She has a law degree, an MA in Catholic theology, and a PhD in ethics and social theory. She is also an avid guitar player and rock music fan who has written extensively on the intersection of popular music, religion, spirituality, and culture.

Dave Perkins, a renowned guitarist and music producer, has worked with a legion of legendary artists, including Ray Charles, Carole King, and Willie Nelson. He received his Bachelor of Arts degree from Georgia College in 1971, majoring in history. After twenty-five years on the road and in the studio as a musician, Perkins earned a Master of Divinity degree and a doctorate from Vanderbilt University. Perkins currently serves as Vanderbilt's associate director of the Religion in the Arts and Contemporary Culture program. He has also released a critically acclaimed blues-rock album, "Pistol City Holiness," and written the score and performed all the music for the 2012 feature film *Deadline*.

Austin J. Roberts is currently a PhD student at Drew University in the Graduate Division of Religion. His academic research centers mainly on the intersection between process theology and continental philosophy of religion, which flows into his interests in ecological theology, science and religion, and radical theology. After spending many years as an active musician, he continues to be interested in the arts, particularly film and music. This has led to his work as an editor and contributor for *Imaginatio et Ratio: A Journal of Theology and the Arts*.

Jeff Sellars, PhD, teaches philosophy, humanities, and religious studies in Northern California and Southern Oregon. His current academic research centers mainly on media and culture as well as the study of popular music, literature, and film.

Bill Walker is a PhD candidate in philosophy of religion at Claremont Graduate University. He holds a Masters of Theological Studies from Truett Theological Seminary and a Bachelors degree in economics from Baylor University. He is also the associate pastor of Saint Peter's Church in Charleston, South Carolina. Previously, Bill has taught classes in theology, ethics, and philosophy as an adjunct professor at the University of the Incarnate

Notes on Contributors

Word in San Antonio, Texas. Drawing on the theology of Hans Urs von Balthasar and the political philosophy of Enrique Dussel, Bill's dissertation examines the doctrine of Christian salvation in the context of globalization and the US-Mexico drug war.

David Zahl is the director of Mockingbird Ministries, and editor-in-chief of the Mockingbird blog (www.mbird.com). He graduated from Georgetown University in 2001 and in 2007 founded Mockingbird, a multimedia platform that seeks to connect the Christian message with the realities of everyday life. He and his wife Cate reside in Charlottesville, Virginia, with their two sons, where David also serves on the staff of Christ Episcopal Church, supervising their ministry to students and young adults. He is a licensed lay preacher in the Episcopal diocese of Virginia, and his first book, *A Mess of Help: From the Crucified Soul of Rock N Roll*, appeared in 2014. Most recently, he coauthored *Law and Gospel: A Theology for Sinners (and Saints)*.

Introduction

JEFF SELLARS

From independent rockers to more mainstream artists, The Beach Boys' music has inspired numerous imitators, emulators, and admirers. The Beach Boys are undeniably one of the most successful rock bands in history. They made it into the Rock and Roll Hall of Fame in 1988 (in the same year as the Beatles) and are included on *Rolling Stone*'s 100 Greatest Artists at number twelve. From the band's humble beginnings in Hawthorne, California in 1961, the band has charted international success, numerous albums, hits, and awards—and artistic acclaim. They have had "thirty-six U.S. Top 40 hits (the most of any U.S. rock band) and fifty-six Hot 100 hits, including four number one singles. . . . According to *Billboard*, in terms of singles and album sales, The Beach Boys are the No. 1-selling American band of all time."[1] But their history is a complicated one—immense personal and musical success tied with abuse, drugs, mental illness, legal fights, and family quarrels, and tragedies. However, punctuating it all, rising above it all, are the beautiful harmonies, the unique stylings, and the musical genius of the group—and in particular Brian Wilson. The continued reverence for him in the alt-rock/indie-rock circuit is proof enough of his endurance and influence as an artist (just one such example being the *Pets Sounds Revisited* tribute album, with various indie artists tackling songs from *Pet Sounds*). Pulsing under this popularity, however, is a spiritual outlook about music and its potential reach.

Brian often talked of religion in general terms, but his early life was shaped by the Christian tradition (this is, of course, not to mention the

---

1. http://www.lyricsfreak.com/b/beach+boys/biography.html.

God Only Knows

general sense of a Judeo-Christian tradition infused in American culture and the era and area of his upbringing). As a young man Brian attended church to avoid his father and train his voice in the choir: "Brian would invite [his friend Ted] Sprague to come to Sunday Services at the Inglewood Covenant Church along with . . . his brothers on Sunday, a ritual he valued both for the emotional succor the sermons offered and the weekly respite from Murry [his father], who had no interest in religion."[2] During the SMiLE sessions, Brian talked of the "essence of all of religion": "I'm very religious. Not in the sense of churches, going to church; but like the essence of all religion. Yeah . . . The essence of *all* religion."[3] Brian's brother Carl was an overtly spiritual person and later become a member (and minister) of the Movement of Spiritual Inner Awareness, a movement that focuses on the teaching of Jesus but also incorporates elements of Buddhism and Transcendental Meditation. Mike Love is a well-known practitioner of Transcendental Meditation.

This book is certainly not an attempt to assert that any of the band members had a deliberate, systematized religious philosophy—or that the Beach Boys necessarily had the particular theological and philosophical concepts found within this book's essays directly in mind when writing and making their music. This book is, instead, a simple search for ripe fruit, where it might be found. But, it is certainly clear that the Beach Boys themselves were aware of a "spiritual" side of their music, and they repeatedly talk about the spiritual nature of their music (and music in general). This is particularly so around the time of *Pet Sounds* and *SMiLE* (and repeatedly echoed down the years as Brian and other band members talked about these projects). The Beach Boys had prayer sessions, for example, before the recording of *Pet Sounds*:

> Brian was developing his spiritual streak, a deeper interest in a supreme being. He'd always considered his music divinely inspired but he was trying to get his mind and soul to a higher plane. . . . He'd begun to pray. It soothed his mind. During the Pet Sounds session, Brian held little prayer meetings. Carl joined him. "Brian would actually write down prayers on paper," Carl recalled. "We'd pray for guidance, to make the most healing sounds." . . . Looking back, Brian said, "God was with us the whole time we were doing

---

2 Carlin, *Catch a Wave*, 18.
3. Priore, *Look! Listen! Vibrate! Smile!*, 167.

Introduction

this record. God was right there with me . . . I could feel that feeling in my head. In my brain."[4]

Carl Wilson also noted the special spiritual side of music in general and the Beach Boys' music in particular:

> Well, the music does have a spiritual quality to it, and it's something we were aware of when we did the sessions—because you'd hear all the sound coming out and it was just an indescribable thing that it did to the environment. You know, you'd be in a room, and you'd hear this noise coming over speakers, and it would be—you know, you'd be resonating with it . . . and of course . . . that's just a basic truth about music is that music is—it's an expression of spirit, and it's a living expression. So it [is] a real people connector because people are spirit.[5]

It is also during the making of *SMiLE* that Brian explicitly stated his musical aims—namely, that with *SMiLE* he was trying to create a teenage symphony to God.[6] There can be little doubt as the opening track of the album, *Our Prayer*, sets the tone for what is to come and explicitly references those aims and echoes his sentiments about music: "'Music is God's voice.' I've often felt that I was on a musical mission, to spread the gospel of love through records."[7]

In addition to this acknowledgment of the spiritual side of their music, there is a clear privileging of innocence, of the childlike, in Brian's music. With *SMiLE* he attempted to make musical innocence (with the help of Van Dyke Parks) through a grand musical and lyrical narrative that circles around ideas of innocence and love. This perceiving and communicating of love and innocence is done in various ways in these recordings. It is done explicitly through the lyrics he and Van Dyke Parks created for *SMiLE*,[8] and it is done through the use of childlike jokes (e.g., the "You're under arrest" joke in "Heroes and Villains" and the use of laughter), as well as in musical arrangement and instrumentation.

Brian's attitude towards music certainly resonates with religious ideas of innocence—for example, Jesus' own apparent privileging of the innocent

---

4. Fusilli, *Pet Sounds*, 96–97.
5. Carl Wilson, "The Beach Boys—The Lord's Prayer."
6. Brian Wilson, "Music is God's Voice."
7. Ibid.
8. For example, on the track "Child is the Father of the Man"—"The Children's song, and the message that they play . . . . The song is love, and the children know the way."

ones—"Jesus . . . said, 'Let the little children come to me, and do not stop them; for it is to such as these that the kingdom of God belongs. Truly I tell you, whoever does not receive the kingdom of God as a little child will never enter it'" (Luke 18:16–17). Brian's privileging of the innocents is summed up beautifully by the lyrics he and Van Dyke Parks created for the *SMiLE* track "Child is the Father of the Man"[9]: "The children's song, and the message that they play . . . The song is love, and the children know the way." This is not just a simple naïve privileging: the "Child of the Man" refrain in *SMiLE* does more to push this argument of a deeper reading than mere words can do. The existential angst and intellectual workings are present in the lyrics of "Surf's Up"—and the hard-won innocence of the refrain is brought about only after this deep, internal argument and exploration of human experience. This deeper philosophy of childlikeness is a musical argument that alerts the perceptive listener that the way into the spiritual life, for Brian, is through this path of innocence. This is clear from Brian's own interpretation of the lyrics of "Surf's Up": "*I heard the Word*—of God; *Wonderful thing*—the joy of enlightenment, of seeing God. And what is it? A *children's song!* And then there's the song itself; the song of children; the song of the universe rising and falling in wave after wave, the song of God, hiding His love from us, but always letting us find Him again, like a mother singing to her children."[10]

Whether it is the deceptively simple, melodic arrangement of a harpsichord in "Wonderful" or the complex workings of a vocal arrangement in "Surf's Up," the push of the music is towards an innocent reception of

---

9. This is, of course, a taking up of "The Rainbow," where William Wordsworth used the same expression:

"My heart leaps up when I behold
 A rainbow in the sky:
So it was when my life began;
 So is it now I am a man;
So be it when I shall grow old,
 Or let me die!
 The Child is father of the Man;
 And I could wish my days to be
Bound each to each by natural piety" (*The Poetical Works of William Wordsworth*, Vol. II, 292).

Brian himself attributed this to Karl Menninger: "And another thing that interests me . . . who was it, Karl Menninger, who said, 'The Child is the father of the man'? That fascinates me!" (Priore, *Look! Listen! Vibrate! Smile!*, 167).

10. Ibid., 89–91.

Introduction

the narrative. Brian is working those arrangements to allow the listener to receive the work as a whole, to have the piece resonate with emotional and intellectual impact, to have the audience understand it and recognize it. Even the title, *SMiLE*, betrays this fact: it is simple, direct, childlike, and brings with it connotations that are recognizable and understandable. There is also the complicated issue of *SMiLE*'s initial reception. Brian's attempt to present his work was thwarted by his fellow bandmates and record company. With the abandonment of the project, one can trace a sense of continued innocence—and the abandonment of *SMiLE* itself can be read as an act of innocence (i.e., the refusal to let it go forward when it failed to be received in innocence by his bandmates and record company can be read as an attempt to save the "purity" of it from such harshness). However, this can also appear as just a "giving up," or possibly as naiveté. Simply because love believes all things does not necessarily mean that it is also deceived. Brian lost his way during the making of the album—to a very large extent due to drug use and psychological issues, but also due to the opposition of the band and record company. When it was not received in love (in the spirit in which it was meant by Brian), he decided to abandon it. And the attempt to create and reveal a spiritual love, the revelation of love revealed within the work of *SMiLE*, could then be said to mirror the perception and revealing of love in general. So the argument goes, if love is to be revealed then this love must be something that the world can recognize—it cannot be purely and wholly other. The inner reality of love is only recognized by love, in the unity of faith, hope, and love—and not only this. If (to paraphrase 1 Corinthians) faith, hope, and love abide, but the greatest of these is love, then, following Kierkegaard, it is "the very ground of everything, exists before everything, and remains when everything else is abolished. Love is therefore the 'greatest' among 'these,' but that which in the sense of perfection . . . is the greatest must also be able to undertake the business of the lesser ones (if I may put it this way) and make them more perfect."[11]

Coupled with this sense of innocence there arises a criticism often leveled against the Beach Boys: namely, that of the Beach Boys being too simplistic (sometimes musically and especially lyrically). Surely, the essays in this collection will make an implicit argument against such a reading of the Beach Boys' music—and with a simple mention of songs, one can begin to see that argument forming. Intricate music and harmonies always abound in their early music and even lyrically there are gems (e.g., just to name a

---

11. Kierkegaard, *Works of Love*, HarperPerennial, 213.

few, "In My Room," "Warmth of the Sun," "Let Him Run Wild," "Warmth of the Sun"). "In My Room" takes on special meaning when considering the genesis of the song—a retreat and re-creation, a spiritualized and protective prayer against the abuse Brian endured as a child and young man and a psychological and existential comment on the state of being. "Warmth of the Sun," to take another example, was written in a direct emotional response to the assassination of JFK. Admittedly, things can be seen as more interesting once Brian collaborates with Tony Asher and especially Van Dyke Parks—and also periodically when, in later years, the rest of the band begins to come into its own (for example, in the development of Dennis Wilson as a songwriter and in the band's rising eco-awareness). But there is a deepness in Brian's (and the band's) simplicity that bears consideration, and, as a consequence, there are questions that require answers: Does simplicity necessarily equate with easy, unrefined, or unthinking? Can there be a beauty and sophistication to simplicity that can transcend the ideas of "naïve" and "uncomplicated"? Moreover, as rock critic and author Anthony DeCurtis puts it, while talking about the song "I Get Around," "It's very easy to be complex and to show off—or to have people think, 'Wow, that's complex!' What's difficult is to be very complex and have every single thing you do have an emotional impact, and have the hearer not even be aware of it—just hear it the first time and get it. That's hard. And that's what Brian Wilson can do. That's what a song like 'I Get Around' can do."[12] Again, I think these essays make just such an implicit argument against an easy reading of the Beach Boys' music.

The approach taken in this collection is in a sense a reflection of all of the above: it is to read the music from a spiritual, philosophical side and to explore freely those themes that our contributors (from their particular philosophical and theological perspectives) find in the music. Additionally, the organization of such an enquiry should be broad enough to allow for this variety (as well as the aforementioned freedom of exploration) but also narrow enough to give a sense of cohesion and focus—as well as allowing for a narrowed and deeper treatment of the Beach Boys' music. Perhaps more important, the Beach Boys' music might lend itself to such an enquiry such as ours: the themes of faith, hope, and especially love are some of the most common, though certainly not the only, themes to be found in their vast catalogue. When we couple this with Brian's mission "to spread the

---

12. DeCurtis, *Brian Wilson: Songwriter 1962–1969*.

Introduction

gospel of love through records"[13] and his sense of music as spiritual—of thinking "pop music is going to be spiritual . . . I think that's what we're going to hear. Songs of faith. Anyhow, that's the direction *I* want to go"[14]—one has a strong case for this being a striking way to explore philosophical and spiritual meanings that might reside in the music and lyrics. As noted above, the topic of the Beach Boys and philosophical and religious readings of their music is a very broad one—one that would have the tendency to get away from a small book project and make it a rambling or slightly incoherent collection of essays. In addition to the aforementioned reasons, we have also decided to use the aegis of faith, hope, and love as a way to group the collection into broad categories. However, this is not an attempt to define the three virtues as evidenced by the Beach Boys' music and lyrics. Rather, it is, in this sense, a means to rally the authors around broad enough themes that still allow for free investigation while having the essays hang together as a set.

But, of course, some warnings should sound here (certainly, much more than can be discussed in this introduction). In music, the experience of the music and lyrics go hand in hand, informing each other, conveying meaning together in concert. There are dangers in separating content and form. The music and lyrics create a world that must be stepped into and experienced and perceived. In writing about music, we might strip the music of this special "content," for example, by focusing just on lyrical matters (and lyrical subjects devoid of the inflections, nuances, variations and performances of the singer or singers) to the detriment of the musical whole. We must be careful in analysis and reception to have this in mind when writing or reading about an auditory form.

Lastly, this book is not an attempt to tame the music, to hold it down, to define it by giving it a once-for-all interpretation—or to be a mere nonmusical intrusion into the heart of the music. The music written about here is a multifaceted, profound conveyor and our interpretation is a process of formation. As Marcel warned, "a music worthy of the name is always laden with truth. Like every expression, music is a restitution, a releasing of what one has breathed in. It can be appreciated only if it is intimately experienced. To appreciate it is first of all to make it your own . . . . [W]hat I fear above all is the intrusion (camouflaged) of non-music in the very

---

13. Brian Wilson, "Music is God's Voice."
14. Priore, *Look! Listen! Vibrate! Smile!*, 167.

God Only Knows

heart of music."[15] I hope we can recognize and respect this openness and hermeneutical process. It is my desire that these musings will be used as a way of sending us back to the music—returning us, with additional energy and stimulation, to the beauty of the music itself, to experience it again, hopefully refreshed and with renewed appreciation.

---

15. Marcel, *Music and Philosophy*, 124.

One

Wonderful Thing

A Children's Song! Brian Wilson, *SMiLE*, and Faith

STEVEN R. GUTHRIE

In 1966, Brian Wilson told journalist Jules Siegel:

"I'm doing the spiritual sound, a white spiritual sound. Religious music. Did you hear the Beatles album? Religious, right? That's the whole movement. That's where I'm going. It's going to scare a lot of people." "Yeah," Brian said, hitting his fist on the desk with a slap that sent the parakeets in the large cage facing him squalling and whistling. "Yeah," he said and smiled for the first time all evening. "That's where I'm going and it's going to scare a lot of people when I get there."[1]

The project Wilson was working on at the time was the album that would come to be known as *SMiLE*, and as this bit of the interview suggests, from the very beginning, Wilson was hoping to do more than write some good pop songs. In the 2011 box set release of *SMiLE*, Wilson writes, "Many years ago I said that 'Music is God's Voice.' I've often felt that I was on a musical mission to spread the gospel of love through records."[2] *SMiLE* emerges

---

1. Siegel, "Goodbye Surfing, Hello God!" Kindle edition, section 5, location 236–40.
2. Wilson, "Music is God's Voice."

from this sense of musical mission. In other places, Wilson has called the album "a teenage symphony to God" and even "a rock opera to God."[3]

It is worth asking then how these spiritual aspirations were realized in the writing and recording of SMiLE. What exactly is involved (or, what did Wilson feel should be involved) in creating a "spiritual sound"? How did the "mission to spread the gospel of love" shape the music on SMiLE? Clearly, Wilson wasn't simply or even primarily interested in writing religious lyrics, or in using texts that have to do with spirituality. He was after a spiritual *sound*. The lyrics to SMiLE in any case would be written, for the most part, by Van Dyke Parks, not Brian Wilson. So then, Wilson's spiritual vision is manifested in the musical material of SMiLE, as well as in the compositional process behind the work.

Wilson's search for a spiritual sound ended up shaping SMiLE in two areas particularly: first, in the increased element of openness and receptivity in the compositional process behind the music; and second, in the album's emphasis on joy and laughter. And while SMiLE is not the product of Christian theological reflection, its emphasis on these two areas reflects some perceptive intuitions that resonate with Christian theology. In particular, the SMiLE recordings and Brian Wilson's understanding of those recordings suggest some profound insights into the distinctive character of faith.

Thinking about Faith

Of the three theological virtues, "faith" may be the most prone to misunderstanding. Three potential areas of confusion are worth mentioning particularly. First, some confusion arises from the fact that in ordinary usage the word *faith* often functions as a metonym for an entire system of belief. So, when we say of someone: "her faith is the most important thing in her life," we aren't referring to the Christian virtue of faith and belief in her life more narrowly. Instead we have in mind the whole network of beliefs, practices, and relationships comprised within her Christian life.

There is a second and similar area of potential confusion, arising from a distinction long been recognized by theologians. *The Catechism of the Catholic Church* observes:

---

3. Lambert, *Inside the Music of Brian Wilson*, 261.

> Faith is a personal adherence of the whole man to God who reveals himself. It involves an assent of the intellect and will to the self-revelation God has made through his deeds and words. "To believe" has thus a twofold reference: to the person and to the truth.[4]

Faith, the Catechism acknowledges, has a "subjective" element (*a personal adherence of the whole person*), and an objective element (an adherence *to God who reveals himself*). Traditionally, theologians have designated this twofold character of faith by the Latin terms *fides qua creditur* (the faith by which it is believed) and *fides quae creditur* (the faith which is believed). The first refers to the subjective element, the "personal adherence of the whole person." The second refers to the objective element, the God and the revelation to which the whole person adheres. In conversations about faith, a failure to recognize these two aspects and the distinction between them may give rise to misunderstanding.

There is a third potential source of confusion; one that arises from how the word *faith* is often used in academic settings, and in debates over the place of religion in education or in the public square. Often, and understandably, such discussions circle around the relationship of "faith" and "reason." This pairing, however, risks suggesting that the essential character of faith is its otherness from reason. We may conclude that the core function and defining character of faith is to offer an alternative to, or even to stand in opposition to "reason."[5] A good example comes from the Harvard cognitive scientist Steven Pinker. In 2006 Harvard issued a review of its General Education requirements. It included a statement about discussions of "faith and reason." Pinker objected to this statement, and particularly, to the suggestion that

> "faith" and "reason" are parallel and equivalent ways of knowing, and [that] we [faculty] have to help students navigate between them. But universities are about reason, pure and simple. Faith—believing something without good reasons to do so—has no place in anything but a religious institution, and our society has no shortage of these.[6]

4. Catholic Church, *Catechism of the Catholic Church*, 54.

5. Of course a further problem with the pairing is that faculty lounge-level discussions of "faith and reason" often begin without a very clear idea of what comprises either. Such conversations in other words often suffer from not only a rather thin conception of faith, but also from a facile conception of rationality.

6. Pinker, "Less Faith, More Reason."

Again, what is notable is that Pinker offers an essentially negative definition of faith. Faith is *just* the absence (or even the rejection of) knowledge. Faith is "believing something without good reason." On this account, faith is epistemically indistinguishable from superstition, drug-induced hallucinations, or paranoid delusions. Even for those who reject belief in God, this seems like an unsatisfying account of faith. Surely, when we tell a friend: "I have faith in you" we are saying something other than: "I believe in you without any good reason."

What then should we mean by "faith" in the discussion that follows, in connection with *SMiLE* and Brian Wilson's songwriting process?

Faith as a general human disposition is marked by an attitude of openness, receptivity, and dependence. To "have faith" or to act in faith is not to feel or act "without reason." Rather, in faith one gladly, willingly, depends, trusts, rests, or relies upon someone or something outside oneself. When I have faith, I feel certain, not because of my exhaustive exploration of some matter, but because of the word of another. When I have faith I am confident of the outcome, not because I have covered every contingency myself, but because the situation is in the hands of one I trust. To have faith is to ground my confidence in something or someone outside myself. In faith I extend beyond myself in openhanded trust and reliance.

On this definition, faith is indeed at odds with "reason"—as it has been defined in the West through much of the post-Enlightenment era. In his 1784 essay, "What is Enlightenment?," Kant declares that

> *Enlightenment is man's emergence from his self-incurred immaturity. Immaturity* is the inability to use one's own understanding without the guidance of another. This immaturity is *self-incurred* if its cause is not lack of understanding, but lack of resolution and courage to use it without the guidance of another. The motto of enlightenment is therefore: *Sapere aude*! [Dare to be wise!] Have courage to use your *own* understanding![7]

The defining character of enlightenment, Kant suggests, is autonomy. Dependence and reliance on others is a mark of immaturity and irrationality. Stringently applied, however, this standard of reason seems more likely to lead to solipsism. We do not better understand a world that is outside and other than us by refusing to learn from or depend upon anyone outside and other than us.

---

7. Kant, *An Answer to the Question: "What is Enlightenment?,"* 1, italics in translation.

Wonderful Thing

Within the Christian sphere specifically, faith is inextricably bound up with the economy of gift, or grace. Indeed, faith is the human disposition that corresponds to God's grace. Grace indicates God's free and open-handed goodness toward humanity, a generosity and benevolence rooted in God's love, rather than in human achievement. Faith in turn is the human response by which men and women rely on what is freely given, rather than on their own resources. John Calvin underlines the connection between faith and grace, writing that "faith arises from God's promise of grace in Christ."[8] So, faith is not simply recognition or even acceptance of truths about God. Calvin observes: "merely to know something of God's will is not to be accounted faith."[9] After all, he continues, "God's word to Adam was, 'You shall surely die.' God's word to Cain was 'The blood of your brother cries out to me from the earth.' But these words are so far from being capable of establishing faith that they can of themselves do nothing but shake it."[10] No, faith in its fullest sense, Calvin argues, involves knowledge of the benevolence and mercy of God, and the certainty that God will freely and generously provide for us:

> Thus, surely, we shall more closely approach the nature of faith; for it is after we have learned that our salvation rests with God that we are attracted to seek him. This fact is confirmed for us when he declares that our salvation is his care and concern. Accordingly we need the promise of grace, which can testify to us that the Father is merciful; since we can approach him in no other way, and upon this grace alone the heart of man can rest.[11]

It is clear from Calvin's discussion that faith in the Christian sense necessarily includes both the subjective and objective dimensions mentioned above. Faith is to rest in and upon another. That means that faith includes the disposition of the believer, even as it is oriented toward the one in whom he believes.

These passages from Calvin also point to two other dimensions of faith that often arise in theological discussion. We might refer to them as the epistemic and the ontological. The former concerns trust and dependence upon another as the condition for knowledge. The latter concerns trust and dependence with respect to ones own being. Faith in the first

---

8. Calvin, *Institutes of the Christian Religion* 3.2.7., 549
9. Ibid., 550.
10. Ibid.
11. Ibid.

sense recognizes that *what we know* is grounded in One outside of ourselves. So Josef Pieper writes,

> "To believe" means to regard something as true and real on the testimony of someone else. Therefore, the reason for believing "something" is that one believes "someone." Where this is not the case, something other than proper belief is involved.[12]

Faith in the second sense recognizes that *who we are*—our being, our worth, and our acceptance—is grounded in One outside of ourselves. Such faith "validates the self precisely as knowing that its source lies somewhere other than in the self."[13] Faith in the first sense (the epistemic dimension) leads to openness and receptivity. Faith in the second sense (the ontological dimension) leads to joy. We will consider each of these in connection to *SMiLE*.

SMiLE and Receptivity

At about the same time Wilson told Siegel he was pursuing a new, "spiritual" and "religious" sound, he also began experimenting with a new method of composition and recording. This method came to be known as Wilson's "modular" approach to recording. Rather than composing complete songs, or even writing blocks of music to be used as "verse" or "chorus" or "bridge," Wilson began bringing musical ideas into the studio, without any clear sense of where they would fit within the finished work. Tony Asher, one of the lyricists for *Pet Sounds*, recalls that Brian "used to go in and record [instrumental] tracks. We didn't know what they were going to be. They didn't even have melodies."[14] Wilson's modular approach to composition was first employed in "Good Vibrations," but the *SMiLE* sessions carried this method even further. Instrumental textures, melodic phrases, vocal parts, chants and shouts, complex harmonic progressions, and sound effects all were committed to tape, with the intention that these would eventually be assembled, layered, combined, and arranged into a complete musical work. "Brian's revolutionary plan was to record the modules as he conceived them, and then later to assemble a whole album by ordering and organizing the modules in a still-to-be-determined way."[15]

---

12. Pieper, *Faith, Hope, Love*, 31.
13. Dillenberger, "Faith," my emphasis.
14. Harrison, "After Sundown," 42. See also Reum, "Lost and Found."
15. Lambert, *Inside the Music of Brian Wilson*, 260.

Wonderful Thing

This "still-to-be-determined" element is particularly important. Wilson, whose relentless perfectionism and control had so often caused friction in the band, had very deliberately introduced openness and contingency into the recording process. There is a new emphasis on receptivity. Wilson now entered the studio *without* everything mapped out and under control. Rather he came to sessions with a "module" (or a "feel" as he called these musical units), and an interest in hearing how these sounds might develop if realized and recorded. According to Alan Boyd, who worked on assembling the 2011 box set *The SMiLE Sessions,*

> Participants and associates who were present in 1966 have all stated that Brian was constantly coming up with new ideas and new ways of putting the pieces together even as he was writing and recording them. One of the remarkable aspects of these musical collages that Brian was constructing is that the fragments themselves were designed to be musically interchangeable. What started out as part of one song could easily be swapped and become part of something else.[16]

In the months that they worked on *SMiLE*, Wilson and his bandmates and the many session musicians they worked with generated a vast amount of recorded music, without having a clear sense of how these pieces would all fit together. Producers who would assemble 2011's *The SMiLE Sessions* recording from the original masters had over seventy-five master reels of tape to work from.[17]

Wilson's attempt to create a spiritual sound coincided with not only a new compositional technique; it also arose at the same time that he began to experiment with LSD.

> "About a year ago I had what I consider a very religious experience," Wilson told Los Angeles writer Tom Nolan in 1966. "I took LSD, a full dose of LSD, and later, another time, I took a smaller dose. And I learned a lot of things, like patience, understanding. I can't teach you or tell you what I learned from taking it, but I consider it a very religious experience."[18]

Of course, many people have associated the use of LSD and other mind-altering drugs with spirituality. The best-known and most influential figures

---

16. Boyd, "Producer's Notes."
17. Ibid.
18. Siegel, "Goodbye Surfing, Hello God!" Kindle Locations 74–76.

God Only Knows

to draw this connection are Aldous Huxley and Timothy Leary—Huxley in *The Doors of Perception*, his report on his mescaline use, and Leary in *The Psychedelic Experience*—his guide to the use of LSD. No doubt, many of those who were part of the 1960s drug culture aspired to nothing more than a good buzz. Others, however—like Huxley, Leary, and Brian Wilson—saw these mind-altering drugs as a route to spirituality and religious experience. Why should LSD be associated with spirituality? What about this drug might lead users to expect religious experiences?

Here again as with Wilson's modular compositional technique, a point of connection is receptivity. The person taking the drug surrenders control in order to move beyond herself (or perhaps, better: she surrenders control in order *to be moved by* that which is beyond herself). So, Huxley speaks of mescaline's potential to facilitate "the universal and ever present urge to self-transcendence."[19] Indeed he writes, "the urge to transcend self-conscious selfhood is . . . a principal appetite of the soul."[20] In the same way, according to Leary, one of the great virtues of LSD is that it removes one's inhibitions, releasing the mind from the impulse to control. "Avoid imposing the ego game on the experience" he advises, in a passage that will later inspire the Beatles' song "Tomorrow Never Knows."

> You must try to maintain faith and trust in the potentiality of your own brain and the billion-year-old life process. With your ego left behind you, the brain can't go wrong. . . . Trust your divinity, trust your brain, trust your companions. Whenever in doubt, turn off your mind, relax, float downstream.[21]

"*Have faith . . . trust . . . trust . . . trust . . .*" Leary writes.[22] Obviously the object of Leary's faith is not the God of Christian belief, but "your divinity." Nevertheless a cornerstone of the transcendent experience he describes is receptivity—surrendering to something beyond or other than one's own rational command.

For Wilson as well, the drug use, the new songwriting techniques, and spirituality didn't just coincide; they were all of a piece. In a number of places Wilson draws connections between his use of LSD, his interest of spirituality, and the writing of *SMiLE*. Wilson recalls that "Good Vibrations"—the

---

19. Huxley, *The Doors of Perception*, 63.
20. Ibid., 20.
21. Leary, *The Psychedelic Experience*, 14.
22. Ibid.

Wonderful Thing

first song on which he employed his new "modular" technique—was inspired by *both* an LSD trip and a profound desire to write spiritual music.

> I'd taken acid for the third and final time. After two bad experiences, this trip was the ultimate in LSD joyrides—everything it was supposed to be, four hours of enlightenment and spirituality . . . "Good Vibrations" was going to be the summation of my musical vision, a harmonic convergence of imagination and talent, production values and craft, songwriting and spirituality. I'd written it five months earlier and imagined the grand, Spectorlike production while on the LSD trip.[23]

When the "Good Vibrations" single was completed, Wilson's vision extended to the recording that would become *SMiLE*.

> I told [Van Dyke Parks] the new album [*SMiLE*] was tentatively titled *Dumb Angel* and explained that my goal was to surpass *Pet Sounds*. Musically and philosophically. I imagined myself creating a whole new form of music, religious, white, spiritual music. In a phrase, I confided to Van Dyke, I was going to attempt to compose what I called "a teenage symphony to God."
>
> Needing to put myself "out there" with God, I started the endeavor by purchasing a couple of thousand dollars' worth of marijuana and hasish, enough to keep me stoned and in the state of mind where I imagined myself being deeply creative and spiritual.[24]

Again, it is worth noting that Wilson draws these same three elements together—spirituality, experimentation with musical form, and drug use. He sets out to create "a teenage symphony to God;" a work that will constitute "a whole new form of music," the composition of which is made possible by the use of drugs.

SMiLE, then, emerges from a striking posture of creative activity, paired with creative receptivity. With respect to Wilson's modular technique, the complete songs emerged not according to a structure worked out in advance, but were drawn together as Wilson listened to the various components and considered their possibilities. The resulting songs, such as "Good Vibrations," are characterized by considerable structural and harmonic complexity, but it is a complexity that arose from an initial receptivity. Wilson, in other words, engaged in a dialogue with the materials,

23. Wilson, *Wouldn't It Be Nice? My Own Story*, Bloomsbury, 144, 145.
24. Ibid., 148.

God Only Knows

in a compositional process of "venturing out," rather than one of "planning out." The music itself exhibits a compositional complexity—a kind of rationality—that arises from receptivity. Likewise, in terms of the creative process, it is Wilson's initial receptivity and venturing out that allowed him to arrive at the rational complexity of the completed work. This suggests a far richer understanding of the relationship between faith and reason than suggested by Pinker or Kant. For Wilson, the venturing out comes first. The result is not blind wandering, but further insight and discovery. The initial venture is the necessary condition of fuller realization.

Theologians will recognize resonances here with the theological principle of *fides quaerens intellectum* (faith seeking understanding). Faith is not the assent given to what is known, but rather the assent that gives rise to the possibility of knowing. In faith we venture out, aware that neither all the facts nor all of the processes are fully under our command. We do in this sense relinquish the sovereignty of our own rational, conscious control. But this does not represent the end or the abandonment of reason. Faith, in the tradition of *fides quaerens intellectum*, is generative. Anselm (with whom the phrase *fides quaerens intellectum* is especially associated) wrote:

> Teach me to seek You, and reveal Yourself to me as I seek, because I can neither seek You if You do not teach me how, nor find You unless You reveal Yourself. Let me seek You in desiring You; let me desire You in seeking You; let me find you in loving You; let me love You in finding You . . .
>
> I do not try, Lord, to attain Your lofty heights, because my understanding is in no way equal to it. But I do desire to understand Your truth a little, that truth that my heart believes and loves. For I do not seek to understand so that I may believe; but I believe so that I may understand. For I believe this also, that "unless I believe, I shall not understand." [Isa 7:9][25]

Faith understood in this way is not the refusal of knowledge, but the ground of knowledge. Faith seeks understanding—that is its orientation, and its *telos*. Likewise, *fides quaerens intellectum* suggests that faith is the prerequisite for true knowledge. Knowledge and discovery begin with faith; and faith is consummated in knowledge and discovery.

The experience of the artist generally, and Brian Wilson's work on *SMiLE* particularly, is one testimony to the generative and epistemically productive character of faith—where faith is understood as a kind of

---

25. Anselm, "Proslogion," 86–87.

venturing out; as receptivity, openness and the surrender of absolute control. We might say that, against Kant, "enlightenment" does not emerge from a kind of closing oneself off ("have courage to use *your own* understanding," Kant urges), but from opening oneself up. Dependence is not the mark of immaturity, but the condition of productivity. The artist's experience is not the only voice testifying to this generative dimension of faith, but it is one of the most compelling.

Perhaps surprisingly, a similar vision of artistic creativity has emerged from a series of recent studies conducted by Charles J. Limb, an associate professor at Johns Hopkins School of Medicine. Limb described his research in a TED talk entitled "Your Brain on Jazz." Limb and his fellow researchers had jazz musicians improvise while their brain activity was monitored by functional magnetic resonance imaging. Limb found that the kind of creativity and spontaneity required for jazz improvisation seems to involve not only the activation of certain parts of the brain, but the suppression of activity in other areas of the brain—in particular, those areas of the brain associated with analysis, reflection, and control.

> The scientists found that a region of the brain known as the dorsolateral prefrontal cortex, a broad portion of the front of the brain that extends to the sides, showed a slowdown in activity during improvisation. This area has been linked to planned actions and self-censoring, such as carefully deciding what words you might say at a job interview. Shutting down this area could lead to lowered inhibitions, Limb suggests.[26]

Another article describing the same research notes that "[i]n addition, the brain regions involved with all the senses lit up during improvisation, indicating a heightened state of awareness—the performers literally taste, smell, and feel the air around them."[27] Here again, it seems that creativity and novelty are encouraged by responsiveness and receptivity rather than simply by control, planning, and deliberative analysis.

I am not suggesting that the Johns Hopkins research or Wilson's *SMiLE* demonstrate an Anselmian vision of faith and reason. I do, however, think that it is significant that when Wilson set out to write "spiritual" music, his intuition was that one dimension of "spirituality" was openness and receptivity. And from the perspective of Christian theology, this intuition is essentially right. In fact, the kind of openness and receptivity that

26. "This is Your Brain on Jazz."
27. Zagorski, "The Science of Improv."

Wilson demonstrates corresponds in important ways to what Christians mean when they talk about faith.

Of course, Christian faith is not just "openness" or "receptivity." It is openness and receptivity to God. As Karl Barth says,

> [i]n Christian faith we are concerned quite decisively with a meeting. "I believe in"—so the Confession says; and everything depends on this "in." ... [W]hat interests me is not myself with my faith, but He in whom I believe.[28]

But this trust in another also suggests why the experience of taking mind altering drugs is ultimately so disillusioning for Wilson, and so unhelpful. Wilson has often spoken about his deep regret at having used LSD. Asked in a 2002 interview, "if he has any regrets[.] [H]e answers quickly, 'Only one—taking LSD. It really fouled up my mind.'"[29]

Genuine openness is openness *to another*. The drug-induced experience in many instances merely represents an openness to one's own subconscious, dimensions of one's own inarticulate experience, or one's immediate and unfiltered impressions. There may be some value to all of this, but it is not, in the richest sense, "openness." Indeed, while drugs like LSD may at one level facilitate openness by allowing one to "turn off your mind, relax, float downstream," they ultimately inhibit receptivity. Those who have spent any time with a person using mind-altering drugs can bear witness that in this state, people generally become less, not more, available to others. The drugged person is less deeply empathetic, less responsive. He is less likely to undertake the demanding journey of self-transcendence necessary to truly see, hear, and perceive the other.

Tragically, LSD opened Wilson to voices which eventually turned dark and destructive. According to a 2011 *Guardian* interview

> LSD wreaked unimaginable havoc on the 25-year-old Brian Wilson. He abandoned *SMiLE* unfinished ... Wilson began hearing voices "saying derogatory things," telling him that he was finished and was going to die soon, a condition that continues to this day. "Every day," he nods. "A daily struggle."[30]

For the Christian, the virtue of faith identifies not only a point of departure ("becoming open"), but a point of destination. It designates not only

---

28. Barth, *Dogmatics in Outline*, 15, 16.
29. O'Hagan, "A Boy's Own Story."
30. Petridis, "The Astonishing Genius of Brian Wilson."

moving beyond the self but moving toward another as the center of one's epistemic universe, the ground of one's confidence and the focus of one's attention.

SMiLE and Joy

Faith is to place one's hope and confidence in another. "So faith means trust" Karl Barth writes. "Trust is the act in which a man may rely on the faithfulness of Another, that His promise holds . . . 'I believe' means 'I trust.'"[31] If our faith rests in another with respect to what may be known or discovered, then (as I have been arguing), the appropriate and reasonable posture is openness, receptivity, and responsiveness. If our faith rests in another with respect to our very being—our worth and our acceptance—then the reasonable and natural response is *joy*.

> I have been made free by Him who can do what I can neither begin nor accomplish of myself . . . . I breathe, and now I breathe joyfully and freely in the freedom which I have not taken to myself, which I have not sought nor found by myself . . . . No more must I dream of trusting in myself, I no longer require to justify myself, to excuse myself, to attempt to save and preserve myself.[32]

In faith, the weight of the worth of my own existence is lifted from my shoulders. I am no longer bent double under its burden, day after day carrying the load of my own value and the validity of my being. Another carries that weight. Those freed from such a burden are now able to run, dance, and—significantly—play. In his essay *Theology and Joy*, Jürgen Moltmann considers the question: Why did God create the world? "This" he writes, "is the question of a child who is no longer a child."[33]

> He has learned that in the adult world everything exists for a good reason . . . . Faith answers the unchildish childhood question in a childlike way; and the wisdom of theology ends with the liberty of the children of God . . . . Anyone who lays hold of the joy which embraces the creator and his own existence also gets rid of the dreadful question of existence: For what? . . . He becomes immune

---

31. Barth, *Dogmatics in Outline*, 18.
32. Ibid.
33. Moltmann, *Theology and Joy*, 39.

also to a society which values and rewards men only in terms of their practical usefulness.[34]

Barth recognizes the natural connection between faith and freedom; faith and joy. Moltmann observes the similar correlation between faith and childlikeness. Life and love and flourishing are not *earned* by the strong; they are *received* by the child. Jesus declares: "Truly I tell you, unless you change and become like children, you will never enter the kingdom of heaven. Whoever becomes humble like this child is the greatest in the kingdom of heaven" (Matt 18:3–4). Faith frees us to be children. It is striking to set this admonition alongside Kant's essay, "What is Enlightenment?" Kant urges men and women to abandon immaturity and trust in their own reason. Jesus urges men and women to be children and trust in God. Kant suggests that this sort of dependence on another is a kind of slavery. But Moltmann points out that precisely because she receives rather than earns the child is *set free*—to play. "Only the innocent, namely children, or those liberated from guilt, namely the beloved, are able to play . . . . Faith is a new spontaneity and a light heart."[35] It is the child who has faith, because the child's trust is not in his own strength, but in the strength and goodness of another. The child is freed for play, for laughter, and for song.

Here too, Wilson in his aspiration to produce spiritual music seemed to intuit an important dimension of faith. Faith means childlikeness. Faith means a surrender of control. For these reasons, faith corresponds to and leads to joy; it leads one to *SMiLE*.

Music theorist Philip Lambert writes that Wilson believed humor could provide "a direct conduit into a kind of spiritual consciousness that would transcend the immediate musical experience. . . . More simply, Brian has been quoted as saying, '*Humor is sacred*, a gift from God.' It's this perspective that led him to rename his album *Smile*."[36]

> To Brian, a state of laughter was a sublime release—a beautiful moment when a person could be happy, open, and fully expressive. Making an album that would put people into a state of laughter would be almost religious in its significance.[37]

---

34. Ibid., 39, 40, 43.
35. Ibid., 52, 53.
36. Lambert, *Inside the Music of Brian Wilson*, 261, my emphasis.
37. Ibid.

Wonderful Thing

Again we might ask—what is religiously significant about laughter? One of Wilson's friends points to a connection we made earlier, between spirituality and openness or surrendering control. Michael Vosse "recalls Brian's views that 'the moment somebody laughed . . . while they're laughing they cannot control themselves. And at that moment, they can have a spiritual experience.'"[38]

Wilson senses a connection not only between laughter and with openness, but between laughter and childlikeness. He draws this out in a remarkable exegesis of the song "Surf's Up," in his *Cheetah* magazine interview with Jules Siegel. Wilson's commentary on the lyric is worth quoting at length.

> At home, as the black acetate dub turned on his bedroom hi-fi set, Wilson tried to explain the words . . . "It's a man at a concert," he said. "All around him there's the audience, playing their roles, dressed up in fancy clothes, looking through opera glasses, but so far away from the drama, from life—'Back through the opera glass you see the pit and the pendulum drawn.' The music begins to take over. 'Columnated ruins domino.' Empires, ideas, lives, institutions—everything has to fall, tumbling like dominoes. He begins to awaken to the music; sees the pretentiousness of everything. 'The music hall a costly bow.' Then even the music is gone, turned into a trumpeter swan, into what the music really is.
>
> "'Canvas the town and brush the backdrop.' He's off in his vision, on a trip. Reality is gone; he's creating it like a dream. 'Dove-nested towers.' Europe, a long time ago. 'The laughs come hard in Auld Lang Syne.' The poor people in the cellar taverns, trying to make themselves happy by singing. Then there's the parties, the drinking, trying to forget the wars, the battles at sea. 'While at port adieu or die.' Ships in the harbor, battling it out. A kind of Roman empire thing.
>
> "'A choke of grief.' At his own sorrow and the emptiness of his life, because he can't even cry for the suffering in the world, for his own suffering. And then, hope. 'Surf's up! . . . Come about hard and join the once and often spring you gave.' Go back to the kids, to the beach, to childhood.
>
> "'I heard the word'—of God; 'Wonderful thing'—the joy of enlightenment, of seeing God. And what is it? 'A children's song!' And then there's the song itself, the song of children, the song of

38. Ibid.

the universe rising and falling in wave after wave, the song of God, hiding the love from us, but always letting us find it again, like a mother singing to her children."

The record was over. Wilson went into the kitchen and squirted Reddi-wip direct from the can into his mouth, made himself a chocolate Great Shake, and ate a couple of candy bars.

"Of course that's a very intellectual explanation," he said. "But maybe sometimes you have to do an intellectual thing. If they don't get the words, they'll get the music . . . He sprawled on the couch and continued in a very small voice. "So that's what I'm doing. Spiritual music."[39]

"The word of God" according to Wilson—the "joy of enlightenment"—is "a children's song." "Their song is love and the children know the way," the lyrics of "Surf's Up" continue. "*That's why* the child is the father of the man." On the path to enlightenment, the child is the one to follow. Wilson's exposition articulates the profoundly "faith-like" character of SMiLE. Once again there is a striking contrast to Kant's contention that enlightenment means abandoning immaturity. For Wilson enlightenment is a children's song. The children's song is the response of simplicity, beauty, joy, and celebration, that grasps and enters into a reality beyond one's grasp.

Wilson's verbal exposition of the lyric is impressive, but his musical exposition of this portion of "Surf's Up" is even more extraordinary. As he says to Siegel: "If they don't get the words, they'll get the music."[40] Beginning with "I heard the sound," there is a rising melody against a descending bass line, a widening harmonic span. The melody soars through three ascending melodic leaps: an upward fifth from F to C above middle C; followed by an upward melodic sixth from G above middle C to E flat. Finally, the tempo broadens out and slows as the melody stretches to its highest point in this section of the song—an ascending sixth from C above middle C to a high A flat, with the words "a children's song." This is the pinnacle of the melody and the lyric. According to Wilson, the children's song celebrates enlightenment and seeing God. It sounds out the joyful, childlike acceptance of God's love.

Like a cyclist cresting a hill and beginning his descent, the tempo now accelerates as the melody circles downward, descending in a long spiraling melisma over the syllable "ahh." This is the part of the melody that Wilson

---

39. Siegel, "Goodbye Surfing, Hello God!" Kindle locations 303–26.
40. Siegel, "Goodbye Surfing, Hello God!" Kindle locations 294–99.

describes poetically as "the song itself, the song of children, the song of the universe rising and falling in wave after wave, the song of God, hiding the love from us, but always letting us find it again, like a mother singing to her children."[41] Wilson spins out measure upon measure of gratuitous melodic elaboration, like the child described by Moltmann—released from self-justification and freed to play. The rest of the Beach Boys enter vocally under Wilson's descending melody, announcing that the child will "show the way." As Wilson draws out more than sixteen bars of this ecstatic, melodic "Ahh!," one is reminded of Augustine's definition of a "jubilate":

> A person who is shouting with gladness does not bother to articulate words. The shout is a wordless sound of joy; it is the cry of a mind expanded with gladness, expressing its feelings as best it can rather than comprehending the sense. When someone is exulting and happy he passes beyond words that can be spoken and understood, and bursts forth into a wordless cry of exultation. . . . An example from common experience will make what I am saying even clearer to you. People who work in the fields are especially given to joyful shouting. Harvesters and grape-gatherers and other fruit-pickers are greatly cheered by a plentiful crop and rejoice over the fecundity and bounty of the earth. In their exultation they sing, and between the words of their songs they interject happy, wordless sounds that express the elation they feel. This is called jubilation, shouting for joy.[42]

Music theorist Philip Lambert is correct to describe "Surf's Up" as "the soul of *Smile*."[43] Indeed, Wilson himself recognized "Surf's Up" as a highlight of his work with Van Dyke Parks. "Van Dyke and I really kind of thought we had done something special when we finished that one," he told Siegel.[44] Not only is it "the sum total of its creators' most profound artistic visions,"[45] it also embodies *in nuce* the spiritual vision of *SMiLE*.

Joy doesn't come from an impressive appearance or keeping exclusive company: "It's a man at a concert, Wilson explains. "All around him there's the audience, playing their roles, dressed up in fancy clothes, looking through opera glasses, but so far away from the drama, from life." Nor does one achieve enlightenment through great influence or extraordinary

41. Ibid.
42. Augustine, *Expositions of the Psalms*, 99–120, 14.
43. Lambert, *Inside the Music of Brian Wilson*, 275.
44. Siegel, "Goodbye Surfing, Hello God!" Kindle locations 294–99.
45. Ibid.

achievement: "Empires, ideas, lives, institutions—everything has to fall, tumbling like dominoes." The man at the concert, Wilson says "sees the pretentiousness of everything." Likewise "the parties, the drinking" and the "ships in the harbor battling it out"—the pursuit of both pleasure and power still leave him with only "'[a] choke of grief.' At his own sorrow and the emptiness of his life." "And then, hope"—Wilson tells Siegel. And that hope is found in becoming a child; in allowing God's song of love to wash over us "like a mother singing to her children."

The point in all of this is not to contend that SMiLE is a work of Christian theology, or that Brian Wilson was attempting to articulate the idea of "faith" as understood in Christian theology. What we have been engaged in in this essay is the ordinary activity of Christian theology: trying to make sense of things in light of the gospel. What Wilson tells us about his work as a composer fits well within a Christian vision of reality. Moreover, his reflections on SMiLE illuminate and enrich some fundamental Christian ideas about the meaning of faith. In creating SMiLE, Wilson recognized a connection between spirituality and childlike joy. Christian theology recognizes this connection as well. Indeed, joy, play, and song can best be made sense of if the world is as the gospel describes it. If the engine of the world is not competition, but grace; if the fundamental impulse of reality is not survival of the fittest, but love—then beauty makes sense. If God is gracious, then we are right to place our trust and confidence, not in ourselves, but in God. We are right then not only to pursue activity, but to cultivate receptivity. In such a world, it makes sense to be like children, because our Father is strong and will sing over us like a mother singing to her children. In such a world one may not only work but play; one may not only earn but receive; one may not only explain, but also sing. In such a world, one may smile.

Two

Emersonian Individualism and the Quest for Wholeness in *Pet Sounds*

THOMAS M. KITTS

Pet Sounds sprang from the preoccupation of Brian Wilson to create pop music that was new, daring, and profound. Through *Pet Sounds*, Wilson pursued the sublime with an energy that can best be understood as Emersonian—which is to say that he seemed to personify the principles of Ralph Waldo Emerson, the mid-nineteenth-century transcendentalist, who gave expression to an American individualism and spirituality that many, then and today, regard as extreme. Wilson's single-minded ambition and need for individual expression gave rise to one of rock music's epic achievements, one without which twentieth-century American music would be greatly diminished.

Pre-*Pet Sounds*

As 1965 drew to a close, Brian Wilson was both exhausted and restless. He felt limited by his record label, his band mates, and pop music's endless cycle of composing, recording, and touring. After an anxiety breakdown just prior to Christmas 1964, Wilson took himself off the road. Yet he wanted to do more than just write and record hit singles, the measuring stick for recording artists at the time. As Keith Richards said, "Singles were all-important then. You put yourself on the line every three months and therefore it had to be distinctive or else."[1] The pressure on bands like the Beach Boys and the Rolling Stones was enormous. Record labels saw albums only as a way to generate further income from the single and they expected albums to be recorded quickly—within days, not weeks—and to round off the hit or hits with covers and fillers. It would not be until 1967 with the Beatles' *Sgt. Pepper's Lonely Hearts Club Band* and other albums (like Jimi Hendrix's *Are You Experienced?* and Cream's *Disraeli Gears*) that the album gained in stature, and, in 1968, outsold singles for the first time.

But by late 1965 Brian Wilson and others knew pop music was changing. Released in late July, Bob Dylan's "Like a Rolling Stone" snarled and pushed for over six minutes in its complete version, challenging pop music's sense of melody and structure and peaking at number two. In September, Barry McGuire's "Eve of Destruction," replete with apocalyptic imagery, soared to number one. Even more significantly, albums were receiving increased attention. In the spring of 1965, Dylan released *Bringing It All Back Home*, with one acoustic and one electric side, and then, at the end of the summer, *Highway 61*, which concluded with "Desolation Row," an eleven-minute epic. In early December the Byrds released *Turn! Turn! Turn!*, a brilliant album with ethereal Beach Boys-like harmonies and twangy twelve-string guitar pickings. Yes, pop music was changing, becoming more complex, inventive, and bold—in short, growing up. And Wilson was listening. On that same release day as *Turn! Turn! Turn!*, The Beatles issued *Rubber Soul*, which sold an amazing 1.2 million copies in its first nine days, surpassing all previous sales records. It was more the music than the sales which struck Wilson. "This album blows my mind because it's a whole album with all good stuff! . . . *Rubber Soul* is a complete statement, damn it, and I want to make a complete statement, too!"[2] Wilson was anxious to compete and respond. And as 1965 drew to a close, the Beach Boys were among the chief competitors of the Beatles.

Almost two years earlier, Capitol Records and the Beach Boys wondered if the band could survive the British Invasion and the squall of Anglomania that swept over American youth. Yet the Beach Boys not

---

1. Brockris, *Keith Richards*, 88.
2. White, *The Nearest Faraway Place*, 251–52.

Emersonian Individualism and the Quest for Wholeness in *Pet Sounds*

only survived, but also prospered with several 1964 hits, including "I Get Around," their first number one, and several other top ten singles ("Fun, Fun, Fun," number five; "When I Grow Up [To Be a Man]," number nine; and "Dance, Dance, Dance," number eight) and four hit albums (*Shut Down Volume 2*, *All Summer Long*, *Beach Boys Concert*, and *The Beach Boys' Christmas Album*). The band had similar commercial success in 1965. "Help Me, Rhonda" supplanted the Beatles' "Ticket to Ride" for the number one spot in May, and "California Girls" was a huge summer smash at number three. The singles led to top-selling albums with *Today!* (number four) and *Summer Days (And Summer Nights!!)* (number two). More importantly, these albums, benefitting from Brian Wilson's time at home, revealed artistic development with their more sophisticated lyrics, complex song structures, and richer productions. However, as *Summer Days* slipped in the charts, Capitol wanted their fall product. Wilson, however, would not be rushed into writing and producing another formulaic Beach Boys hit.

Capitol was at least somewhat understanding, but the label would not allow the fall and Christmas season to pass without a new Beach Boys' single and album. Since a live album, a usual quick-fix option, had been released a year earlier, Capitol recommended a greatest hits package, which the band rejected, afraid that such a summation might suggest that the band was drying up—especially since the Beatles were still releasing new material. They reached a solution when one of the Beach Boys, no one remembers who, came up with the concept of a Beach Boys party album. The band would record themselves in a party atmosphere, complete with chatter, clinking glasses, sing-alongs, hand claps, bad jokes, and overall lightheartedness. With the exception of Brian's bass guitar, all instruments would be acoustic. The concept made sense: the Beach Boys were a sing-along band; the album satisfied Capitol's hunger for material; the fans would hear the band in a more relaxed setting and attend, however vicariously, a party with them; the album hardly stressed the band's sensitive leader and his increasingly fragile psyche, and, most importantly, it bought Wilson time to plan the band's direction. After a few rehearsals and over a few sessions in a recording studio with friends, wives, and girlfriends along, the Beach Boys had recorded *Party!*, an album of 1950s and '60s favorites. A joyous, fun-filled romp, with musically questionable choices, *Party!* seems to celebrate the band's survival, even victory, over the invading British, who were now with notable exceptions in retreat. With no anxiety of competition, the Beach Boys covered three Beatles songs, including "You've Got to Hide Your

Love Away," sung by Dennis Wilson in a gutsy performance. However, the band, or at least Mike Love, did demonstrate some anxiety in their cover of Dylan's "The Times They Are A-Changin,'" as Love detracts from Alan Jardine's faithful rendering with inane parodic techniques.[3]

Released in early November 1965, *Party!* proved the ideal Christmas release. As a sales promotion, Capitol provided record dealers with one million bags of Beach Boys potato chips to be given away with the purchase of the album—a gesture of confidence and good faith from Capitol, which almost two years earlier had diverted promotional dollars from the Beach Boys to the Beatles. *Party!* sold beyond expectations, peaking at number six with the single "Barbara Ann," a cover of a song first released in 1961, then reaching number two. Brian Wilson, however, was alone in not celebrating the album's commercial success. "The party-time music, while fun, was a throwback to the Beach Boys' old material ... it was definitely out of sync with what I wanted to do. I was heading in a much different direction and, whether the Beach Boys liked it or not, I was taking them with me."[4]

Inspired by the artistic developments in rock music over the past year, Wilson was anxious not just to respond to his competitors, but also to surpass and challenge them. "My real ambition," he said, "was to redraw the entire map of pop music. I wanted to move off the charts and onto a higher plateau."[5]

The Emerging Self

In the years leading up to *Pet Sounds*, Wilson had been increasing assertive. While frequently shy and insecure, in 1963 at age twenty-one, he had petitioned Capitol Records and won creative control for the Beach Boys. Wilson and the band were free to write, produce, and release what they wanted without corporate interference—at least theoretically and legally. Capitol had no regrets as long as Wilson produced hits. In 1964, with similar assertiveness and after years of absurd competitiveness and tension,

---

3. Love does not seem as if he wants to perform the song, jokingly referring to it as a "test song,"—not as in *protest* but as in *test*. For instance, after Jardine sings "drenched to the bone," Love and the audience shout "drench"; after "sink like a stone," "glub"; after "prophesize with your pen," "write." Alan Jardine, who initiated the song, carries on in earnest.

4. Wilson, *Wouldn't It Be Nice*, HarperCollins, 126.

5. Ibid., 126–27.

Emersonian Individualism and the Quest for Wholeness in *Pet Sounds*

Wilson confronted his father, the manager of the Beach Boys. By all accounts, Murry Wilson was petty, abusive, and tyrannical, and especially overbearing in the studio. The band frequently tried to schedule recording sessions to escape Murry, and, when that proved impossible, engineer Chuck Britz rigged up a disconnected control panel, which gave Murry the illusion of producing. The tension exploded during the recording of "I Get Around," when an intoxicated Murry raged on about the weak material and the heartless, self-indulgent stars. Prodded by the band, Brian fired his father. Not completely defeated, Murry connived to wrestle ownership of Sea of Tunes Publishing from Brian through forgeries and a relentless barrage of threatening and guilt-inducing phone calls to his son.[6]

As he began planning *Pet Sounds*, Brian determined not to rely on formulaic Beach Boys hits and themes of innocence, or as he put it, "fun, sun, and bikini-clad buns."[7] He could no longer write convincingly of the Beach Boys myth—happiness was no longer as close as the nearest beach. In a sense, he had gone to the ends of the Western frontier and, if he were to surpass his musical competition, he needed more territory to explore. Never very political, he looked inward to give his work authority. "I was obsessed with explaining, musically, how I felt inside. This, I thought, could be the beginning of a new type of sophisticated-feeling music."[8] This would prove no easy task for one who suffered anxiety attacks, had recently fired his father, felt pressured to create hits, and had begun smoking marijuana heavily and experimenting with LSD as part of his quest for self-discovery.

With the Beach Boys away on a world tour, Wilson began writing *Pet Sounds* in earnest in January 1966. He hired Tony Asher, a jazz pianist now working in advertising, to translate his inner turmoil into lyrics, or in Blakean terms, Wilson's songs of innocence into songs of experience. On a leave of absence from his day job, Asher tolerated Wilson's unpredictable behavior and drug use, and remembers long hours of deep conversation that helped him develop the lyrics. "The general tenor of the lyrics was always his," said Asher. "I was really just his interpreter."[9]

6. Ibid., 363, 97, 121.
7. Ibid., 140.
8. The Beach Boys, *Pet Sounds*, liner notes, 5.
9. Ibid., 9.

God Only Knows
Wilson's Quest for Aesthetic Wholeness and Spirituality

Wilson not only wanted to make a "complete statement" with *Pet Sounds*, but he also wanted to feel complete, to feel whole as well. To Emerson, "it is dislocation and detachment from the life of God that makes things ugly," but it is the poet who "re-attaches things to nature and the Whole ... [and] by a deeper insight—disposes very easily of the most disagreeable facts."[10] Consider how Wilson affirms Emerson in his quest for self-discovery and as he explains the coupling of dark themes and rich melodic structures on *Pet Sounds*: "I find it possible to spill beautiful melodies in moments of great despair."[11] And, "I just wanted the music to sound *whole*, to convey the timeless, emotional content inherent in great works of art—paintings, poetry, symphonies. What I've always described as the presence of God."[12] This insistence on wholeness explains Wilson's preoccupation with vocal harmonizing, symmetry, structure, and what might be called an accessible beauty. His aesthetic contrasts directly with the loose jams, guitar solos, distortions, and the volume of the emerging psychedelic rock of 1966.

Like Emerson, who left the Unitarian church, Wilson developed his spirituality independent of organized religion. "I just believe in Jesus Christ," said Wilson, "but I don't know what religion I am."[13] Emerson found his church in nature, where he said he could transform himself into a "transparent eye-ball" and lose his self-absorption and allow "the currents of the Universal Being [to] circulate through" him.[14] "By such abandonment to the nature of things," the artist finds "that beside his privacy of power as an individual man, there is a great public power on which he can draw, by unlocking, at all risks, his human doors, and suffering the ethereal tides to roll and circulate through him." Then, "His speech is thunder, his thought is law, and his words are universally intelligible."[15] For Wilson, "the studio was like a church" where he sought the artistic authority Emerson described. Sounding almost ministerial, Wilson said he strives to create "music that helps and heals, because I believe music is God's voice."[16] Dur-

---

10. Emerson, "The Poet."
11. *The Making of* Pet Sounds, booklet, 7.
12. Wilson, *Wouldn't It Be Nice*, HarperCollins, 133.
13. Cody, "Brian Wilson, The Beach Boys' Musical Genius."
14. Emerson, "Nature."
15. Emerson, "The Poet."
16. Wilson, *Wouldn't It Be Nice*, HarperCollins, 137.

Emersonian Individualism and the Quest for Wholeness in *Pet Sounds*

ing sessions for *Pet Sounds*, Brian said he and his brother Carl would pray "for light and guidance.... We kind of made [the recording of the album] a religious ceremony."[17] Carl recalled that "Brian would actually write down prayers on paper."[18]

One means that Wilson sought the "Universal Being" and the opening of "his human doors" was through drugs, first marijuana and then LSD. "Grass had given me added creativity, but LSD, though I didn't know it yet, was giving me colors to paint with."[19] Wilson was introduced to LSD by Loren Schwartz, an assistant at the William Morris Agency, who, Wilson said, had an "evangelistic quality" and who "unlocked the doors of perception for me,"[20] echoing both Emerson and the Blakean phrase from which the Doors took their name. On his first of what he says were three trips—there is reason to suspect more—Wilson said he saw "God" and, in a later trip, found "enlightenment and spirituality." But Wilson quickly added, "It scared the shit out of me."[21] Emerson did not condone but understood the artist's use of intoxicants, which "add this extraordinary power to [an artist's] normal powers . . . and help him escape the custody of that body in which he is pent up." However, he concludes, "the spirit of the world, the great calm presence of the Creator . . . [t]he sublime vision comes to the pure and simple soul in a clean and chaste body."[22]

The *Pet Sounds* sessions for Wilson were in no small part mystical. He believed he had experienced what Emerson called "the ethereal tides" or the "currents of the Universal Being" circulating through him. "During the production of *Pet Sounds*," he recalled, "I dreamt I had a halo over my head. This might have meant that the angels were watching over [me]."[23] Consider his description of listening to a playback of "God Only Knows": "magical, beautiful . . . the different sounds bleeding into one [an]other producing a rich, heavenly blanket of music."[24] Furthermore, Wilson said,

---

17. The Beach Boys, *Pet Sounds* liner notes, 17, 11. The "God's voice" quotation was originally stated at the ceremony inducting the Beach Boys into the Rock and Roll Hall of Fame, January 1988.

18. Fusilli, *Pet Sounds*, 97.

19. Wilson, *Wouldn't It Be Nice*, HarperCollins, 119.

20. Ibid., 116.

21. Ibid., 144, 118.

22. Emerson, "The Poet."

23. The Beach Boys, *Pet Sounds* liner notes, 5.

24. Wilson, *Wouldn't It Be Nice*, HarperCollins, 139.

"God was with us the whole time we were doing this record. God was right there with me. I could see—I could feel that feeling in my head. In my brain."[25] Wilson was confident, despite what anyone would say, that he could reach the sublime with *Pet Sounds*, creating a complete statement: emotional, musical, intellectual, and spiritual.

Opposition

From its inception, *Pet Sounds* was more of a Brian Wilson album than a Beach Boys album. Wilson hired Hal Blaine's illustrious Wrecking Crew to record the backing tracks while the Beach Boys were on a world tour. It was the first and only Beach Boys album on which the members did not play instruments. Furthermore, Wilson did most of the lead vocals on *Pet Sounds*, explaining that "I needed to get his one album out to my fans and the public from my heart and soul."[26]

The album, recorded from January through April 1966, cost $70,000[27] to produce (about $500,000 in today's dollars), a then exorbitant expense and length of time to record an album. But Wilson was determined to get the sound he wanted, and, for "God Only Knows," for example, he employed twenty-three studio musicians to play simultaneously. The Beach Boys returned from touring, and as Wilson put it, "filled out the album and we had a classic on our hands."[28] David Leaf accurately compared Wilson's work on *Pet Sounds* to that of an auteur, in the cinematic sense.[29] Wilson is not just the controlling force, but really the only force behind *Pet Sounds*, a work stamped with his vision, style, and obsessions. He seemed to be following Emerson's dictates: "Insist on yourself, never imitate" and "Trust thyself: Every heart vibrates to that iron string."[30] Wilson was relentless in his "single-minded pursuit of a personal vision."[31]

"All my friends thought I was crazy to do *Pet Sounds*"[32]—including most of his fellow Beach Boys, especially Mike Love. Returning from a

25. The Beach Boys, *The Pet Sounds Sessions* liner notes, 2.
26. The Beach Boys, *Pet Sounds* liner notes, 5.
27. See Gaines, *Heroes and Villains*, 146.
28. The Beach Boys, *Pet Sounds* liner notes, 5.
29. Ibid., 19. See also the Beach Boys, *Good Vibrations* liner notes, 35.
30. Emerson, "Self-Reliance."
31. Wilson, *Wouldn't It Be Nice*, HarperCollins, 140.
32. The Beach Boys, *Pet Sounds* liner notes, 14.

Emersonian Individualism and the Quest for Wholeness in *Pet Sounds*

world tour in which they had played Beach Boys hits to vibrant sellout crowds, the band, along with Capitol, had expected more of the typical Beach Boys fare. Instead, they heard introspective lyrics, orchestral arrangements with unusual tempo changes that would rise, pause, and ruminate before progressing tentatively forward, very unlike the steady energy of a pop song. On top of these arrangements, they were to add lead vocals and soaring harmonies. They needed convincing. Tony Asher recalls, "The group was less than enthusiastic about the material. They, along with many others, were hoping and expecting more of what had been hits for them all along . . . . At that point in the music business, the conventional wisdom was that you keep doing what's selling . . . . So they didn't see the wisdom in changing the 'formula.'"[33] Wilson was upset: "I'd pour my soul into these songs . . . . They just wanted me to crank out the songs like a machine . . . . I felt misunderstood, hurt, alienated. Rejected."[34] But Wilson was willing, as Emerson wrote, to "shun mother, father, sister, brother, when our genius calls," realizing that "the virtue in most request is conformity" and "for nonconformity the world whips you with its displeasure."[35] Ironically, stage front man Mike Love provided Wilson with the album's title. During one session, as Wilson pressed the band to strike just the right pitch, Love snapped, "Who's gonna hear this shit? The ears of a dog."[36] The ears and the "pet sounds" were, of course, Brian's, a metaphor he literalizes by including barking dogs at the end of the album.

The music eventually won the band over, but Capitol Records proved less supportive. They did not want to release *Pet Sounds*. Years later, Al Couri, one-time head of promotion at Capitol sounded apologetic for his label's lack of faith in *Pet Sounds*, seeming to equate Wilson's creativity with what record companies fear from artists—unpredictableness: "You've got to understand that Brian was so impulsive, compulsive, you never knew what was coming next."[37] At one meeting scheduled for executives to press Wilson into withholding *Pet Sounds*, Wilson entered with a tape recorder and proceeded to respond to questions only through one of eight prerecorded tape loops—"no comment," "yes," "no," "Can you repeat that?"

33. "Tony Asher Interview."
34. Wilson, *Wouldn't It Be Nice*, HarperCollins, 140, 141.
35. Emerson, "Self-Reliance."
36. Wilson, *Wouldn't It Be Nice*, HarperCollins, 140.
37. Gaines, *Heroes and Villains*, 149.

etc. Exasperated, Capitol kept its commitment to the Beach Boys' artistic freedom and released the album.

The Wholeness of *Pet Sounds*

Wilson and Tony Asher have commented repeatedly that *Pet Sounds* has no narrative, and it doesn't. However, *Pet Sounds* does have a concept: the expression of the internal feelings and thoughts of a complex controlling consciousness through "sophisticated-feeling music." As a result of this ambitious concept, the album is unified in a way that, say, a sonnet sequence of Petrarch or Shakespeare might be. The songs reflect Brian Wilson's emotional state at a particularly ambitious, introspective, and vulnerable time. He wanted to create music to heal himself and any needy listeners. By the time of the recording, Wilson had lost his faith in the healing powers of the beach or in the isolation of his room—see "In My Room" (1963, number 212 on *Rolling Stone's* list of the 500 greatest songs of all time). To be precise, it wasn't, for Wilson, so much the music that healed, but the *making* of the music that healed. As he said, the recording studio became his church and his sanctuary, a place where he was in control and comfortable. Listening to the sessions for *Pet Sounds* reveals Wilson to be not only in control but also enthusiastic and jubilant even as he struggled for just the right sounds.

The power and internal logic of *Pet Sounds* derives from this concept of "sophisticated-feeling music" and the following unifying factors:

1. Emotional expression of the controlling consciousness. Anxious to "directly express [his] feelings," Wilson with Asher did not write simple songs of loss.[38] These are songs infused with pain, but a pain not from a teen breakup or sentimental pop cliché—instead a pain that comes from something deeper: a loss of innocence and a loss of vision and hope that was built from that innocence. The controlling consciousness is questioning the direction of his life. All the lyrics are written in the first person and all, including "Sloop John B.," reveal the consciousness of not only the voice in the song, but also, more importantly, the consciousness behind the album, who is, of course, Brian Wilson—brooding, Byronic, contemplative, and sometimes self-pitying.

---

38. The Beach Boys, *Pet Sounds* liner notes, 5.

Emersonian Individualism and the Quest for Wholeness in *Pet Sounds*

2. Downward movement of that consciousness. *Pet Sounds* begins with hopefulness in "Wouldn't It Be Nice," although, as "wouldn't" signals, that hopefulness is tentative. However, from there the emotional tenor of the album moves downward with only a few brief upturned moments of hope, but the hope never approaches the exuberance of the opening track. The tone and the controlling consciousness moves fairly steadily into despair, concluding with the bleak "Caroline No," in which the final sung word on the album is "no."

3. Musical structures and arrangements. Wilson used song structures, arrangements, instruments, and sound to support his concept. "I wasn't just entertaining people, I was speaking directly to them, directly from my heart."[39] Most of the songs use a common pop structure, a pattern which includes an intro, verse, chorus, and bridge. However, the songs do not progress steadily forward like most pop songs; they often pause at the bridge, quieting as they eliminate instruments, reflective of a ruminating consciousness who pauses before moving forward. Throughout the album and always purposefully, Wilson imposes lush orchestrations within the structures, and employs un-rock and roll instruments like flutes, banjos, harpsichords, and guiro, in addition to sound effects derived from sleigh bells, bicycle bells, water bottles, locomotives, and much more. Yet, amazingly, songs and album never seem cluttered or self-indulgent. Indeed, the overall effect is profound, strikingly harmonic and absolutely riveting while also troubling and then therapeutic for composer and listener.

In short, Wilson has achieved the wholeness which he strove, transforming torment into a great work of beauty, spirituality, and meaning. Rare for a pop record, *Pet Sounds* reaches a moving and dark sublimity.

The Songs

"Wouldn't It Be Nice"

"Wouldn't It Be Nice" could only open *Pet Sounds*. The singer, who could be identified as a young man, perhaps slightly older than the singer in "Be True to Your School," is full of youthful optimism with faith in the couple and love, the promise of adulthood, and institutions like marriage. Any danger

---

39. Wilson, *Wouldn't It Be Nice*, HarperCollins, 140.

of the song being overly sentimental is dispelled by its unique instrumentation, its tempo, its context on the album, and the convincing lyrics and sincerity of the vocals. Indeed, the song is one of the album's masterpieces.

After its dreamlike intro with harp-like guitars (which recur throughout the song), an echoing drum pounds and the song races forward, reflective of the young couple's impatience and desire to make time run. Expressions of love are, of course, almost always mawkish to the outsider, but the buoyancy of the singer, the good-night scene, and the simple childlike vocabulary ("nice," "happy times," "never ending") capture the excitement of youthful love. Notice the eagerness in the use of "and": "Maybe if we think *and* wish *and* hope *and* pray it might come true." In the bridge, often the darkest part of songs on *Pet Sounds*, the couple expresses both a cheerful optimism and conservatism as they give rest to any impulsiveness. Here, Mike Love takes over the vocals from Brian as the music slows and the singer makes a gentle allusion to marriage and sex: "Baby, then there wouldn't be a single thing we wouldn't do." The song draws to a conclusion with the tempo resuming and the contented lovers wishing each other a series of "good nights" and "sleep tights."

However, the singer's joyful love and exuberant hopefulness barely survive the song. As a result, "Wouldn't It Be Nice" deepens every other song on *Pet Sounds*. "I'm Waiting for the Day," for instance, becomes more desperate; "I Just Wasn't Made for These Times" becomes more brooding, and "Caroline No" more bitter.

"You Still Believe in Me"

After the "good nights" and "sleep tights" fade from "Wouldn't It Be Nice," the tone shifts as an ominous intro opens "You Still Believe in Me," an intro created as one musician played twelve quarter notes on the piano's keyboard while another simultaneously plucking the strings inside the piano, creating a high pitched hum like that of a theremin—which was often used in horror and suspense films of the 1950s and which Wilson uses on "I Just Wasn't Made for These Times" and, more famously, on "Good Vibrations." Brian sings lead in repentant tone, acknowledging that he has failed to live up to his girl's love, patience, and faith. The fall into despair has begun.

The brief, cut notes of the harpsichord-like piano twinkle as if in a child's lullaby.[40] In contrast, however, the plaintive brass section and the

---

40. Asher and others insist it is a piano. See *Making of* Pet Sounds, 43; Lambert, *Inside*

Emersonian Individualism and the Quest for Wholeness in *Pet Sounds*

bass form a pattern that rises for three quarter notes before crashing. The effect undercuts the gentleness of the piano and finger cymbals and, along with the vocals and lyrics, reveals a troubled mind struggling to stay afloat. At approximately the 1:30 minute mark, just before the conclusion, a bicycle bell rings three times, signaling perhaps the end of childhood and the encroachment of the adult world and responsibility. The last almost fifty seconds of the song develop from the lyrics' final line of "I wanna cry," as the singer lifts, drops, and twists the last vowel sound into what seems an elongated sigh of regret. One unidentified musician said in reference to this track, "[Wilson's] progressions are always going up, then pausing before they go up again, like they're going toward God."[41]

"That's Not Me"

In "That's Not Me," after a failed quest to fulfill his dreams and discover his identity, the singer returns to his suburban home, seeking the solace of his family and girlfriend and the completion of the expressed promise of "Wouldn't It Be Nice." He tells his love that he is glad he ventured off because "now I'm that much more sure that we're ready." But the singer is not ready; he still hasn't discovered who he is, only, as the title indicates, who he is not. One of the failures of the controlling consciousness of the album is that he never figures out who he is, which dooms his relationships and his quest for self-fulfillment and contentedness. Nevertheless, it is this quest and his resulting torment that drive the album. On this track, the fat bass, the rumbling drums, and the pointed lead guitar lines all emphasize the internal restlessness and self-doubt of the singer and prove more revealing than the self-delusional and self-assured lyrics, delivered effectively by Mike Love.

"Don't Talk (Put Your Head on My Shoulder)"

"Don't Talk" is a desperate attempt for the singer to reinvigorate a failing relationship. Nothing in the lyrics or music suggests the relationship can be saved. The singer pleads with his love in Brian's tender vocals, "don't talk," and to, instead, "listen" to their hearts. But it seems the heart cannot

---

the Music, 230–31.
    41. The Beach Boys, *The Pet Sounds Sessions* liner notes, 14.

overcome the disappointments and heartaches, apparent not only in her potential words, which the singer silences, but also, as the singer tells us, in her "sighs" and "eyes." Unlike in "Wouldn't It Be Nice," where the singer anticipates a bright future, here the singer wants to "live forever tonight" and "not think about tomorrow." The ominous percussion and bass and the mournfulness of the strings suggest the relationship will end shortly. With "Caroline No," "Don't Talk" might be the saddest song on the album, but illustrative of Brian's capability to create "beautiful melodies [for] moments of great despair."[42]

"I'm Waiting for the Day"

"Waiting for the Day" conveys the emotional instability and confusion of a singer in the throes of unrequited love. In three and a half minutes, through several tempo and key changes and vocal tones, Wilson expresses the range of emotions of a forlorn singer who strives to seem rational, balanced, and understanding, but ultimately proves anxious, jealous, frustrated, and frighteningly aggressive. The track opens with echoing timpani blasts, which reflect "a throbbing, aching heart,"[43] before flutes and an almost carousel-like organ soften the tone. The seemingly calm singer courts his lover as an English horn doubles the vocal lines and a ukulele adds some neat fills. Later, after several "yin-yang" shifts,[44] the energy yields for twelve beats to a brooding melancholic string section before the timpani announces the song's final movement in which the singer erupts with five sneering vocal lines, all beginning with "You didn't think . . .".

"Let's Go Away for Awhile"

The aptly titled "Let's Go Away for Awhile" provides a kind of respite, a pregnant pause, from the emotional turbulence of the controlling consciousness. There is no definable melody on the instrumental, which caused Wilson to dare listeners: "Try to hum it."[45] The track holds together through a fairly steady and slow rhythm built primarily on a strumming

---

42. The Beach Boys, *Good Vibrations* liner notes, 27.
43. Lambert, *Inside the Music*, 242.
44. Bruce Johnston's description, *Making of Pet Sounds*, 32.
45. The Beach Boys, *Pet Sounds* liner notes, 11.

Emersonian Individualism and the Quest for Wholeness in *Pet Sounds*

guitar, electric keyboard, a slow booming electric bass line, and Hal Blaine's soft drum pattern. Strings and saxophones rise and fall with occasional and brief lead lines emerging on violin and guitar.

"Sloop John B."

Many have argued that "Sloop John B." should not have been included on *Pet Sounds*. Kingsley Abbot has said that the track "has no lyrical or mood connection with the rest of the album," and Alan Jardine, who suggested the song to Wilson, said, "I think 'Sloop John B.' is a fantastic production, but in hindsight, it probably doesn't fit on that album."[46] As a way to boost sales of *Pet Sounds*, Capitol may have lobbied for the inclusion of the West Indies folk song, which rose to number three on the US singles charts after its late March release. Yet, I argue that "Sloop John B." fits both lyrically and musically on the album. Indeed, its arrangement is an elaborate as any other track. Philip Lambert summarizes his analysis: "The treatment of instruments and rhythms and textures and vocal lines gives the entire arrangement a compelling shape and grandeur."[47]

In search of adventure, a young and innocent singer goes off to sea with his grandfather as a glimmering glockenspiel reflects the ebbs of the ocean. Yet all the singer finds is disorder and recklessness: drunken brawls, police harassment, and a cook's bullying. Like the singer in "That's Not Me," he feels "broke up" and longs to return home, and like the singer in "I Just Wasn't Made for These Times," he yearns to fit in somewhere. Quest ending in disappointment, along with lost love and lost innocence, is one of the major themes of *Pet Sounds*. Interestingly, during the bridge, instead of a sparse musical rumination like most of the other tracks, the vocals continue a cappella, intensifying the singer's desperation.

"God Only Knows"

With accordions and keyboards setting the tempo, the French horn the somber tone, and sleigh bells and clip-clop percussion the rhythm, one of the most ambiguous and sophistical love songs begins. "I may not always love you," sings Carl Wilson, on the album's second masterpiece. Asher

---

46. Abbot, *The Beach Boys' Pet Sounds*, 184. Jardine, quoted in Granata, *Wouldn't It Be Nice*, 114.
47. Lambert, *Inside the Music*, 215.

had to convince Brian to keep the line. "Brian, that's real life," he argued.[48] Indeed, the song has none of the hyperbole generally associated with love songs, but it may explain Brian's tumultuous marriage to Marilyn. In the subsequent lines, the singer explains that his love will last as long as the stars are above her. Not to overthink the image, but are the stars above us during the daylight? Is Wilson suggesting that love is here one instant and gone the next—as he proclaims in "Here Today"? The singer in "God Only Knows" cannot explain his love. Only God, he explains, can fathom his complicated emotions, which, throughout the album—excepting "Wouldn't It Be Nice"—involve a mixture of love, uncertainty, dependency, self-doubt, turmoil, and more. In fact, by the second track, "You Still Believe in Me," the controlling consciousness has lost all his certainty in love and self. The singer *wants* and may even *need* to love, but is unsure whether he *can* love, torn by some kind of "primal antagonism," as Emerson called it, that very much leads to his instability and discomfort.[49] In several songs, the singer is neither content in love or out of love ("Don't Talk," "Here Today"), at home or away from home ("That's Not Me," "Sloop John B.").

In "God Only Knows," as throughout *Pet Sounds*, the bridge suggests the singer's troubled consciousness and inability to move forward. In the very center of the song right on the heels of the second verse, the bridge halts the clip-clop rhythm and silences the accordions and horns, as we hear only staccato strings and a potent bass punctuated by a drum roll. The effect is haunting and furthers the desperation and uncertainty. After repeating the second verse, the tracks draws to a close with not the singer's proclaiming his love but his dependency, as "God only knows what I'd be without you"—with Brian and Bruce Johnston joining Carl on the vocals. A song of great desperation, ambiguity, fear, and prescience, "God Only Knows" suggests the awareness of the controlling consciousness that all of his love relationships might be doomed. Indeed, none of the remaining tracks offers hope in love. In a biographical note, Brian and Marilyn would divorce in 1979, despite Marilyn's devotion to Brian and her tolerance of his erratic behavior.

Paul McCartney has often acknowledged "God Only Knows" as one of his favorite songs. On the BBC's Radio 1 during its fortieth anniversary celebration, he said it is "one of the few songs that reduces me to tears every

---

48. Wilson, *Wouldn't It Be Nice*, HarperCollins, 139.
49. Emerson, "The Conservative."

Emersonian Individualism and the Quest for Wholeness in *Pet Sounds*

time I hear it."[50] The song's power derives from several sources, but not to be overlooked is Carl's heartfelt but subtle vocals, expressing melancholy, vulnerability, and a range of emotions and fears without resorting to what Jerry Wexler called "oversouling." In fact, nowhere on the album do any of the vocal performances resort to oversouling or "gratuitous and confected melisma" and "flagrantly artificial attempts [to] substitute [vocal pyrotechnics] for real fire and passion."[51]

"I Know There's an Answer"/ "Hang on to Your Ego"

Mike Love refused to sing "Hang on to Your Ego," which he called a "doper song,"[52] until the lyrics to the chorus were reworked and the title changed to "I Know There's an Answer." Rather than further aggravate Love, Brian agreed. The change adds a moment of at least slight confidence to the controlling consciousness since there seems to be a potential answer to his various dilemmas, albeit one hard to find. With "Hang On to Your Ego," however, the singer proclaims that he will "lose the fight" for identity and self-esteem and, thus, his downward spiral quickens. None of the idiosyncratic instrumentation or rhythms changed with the lyrics as Wilson makes use of a banjo, keyboard, and tambourine that creates tension playing off the two bass guitars and blaring saxophones.

"Here Today"

A drastic contrast has occurred in the controlling consciousness between "Wouldn't It Be Nice" and "Here Today," perhaps the most bitter and cynical song on *Pet Sounds*, delivered as Mike Love's best performance on the album. The singer presents himself as the voice of experience. He calmly and rationally warns a new lover that the course of love moves quickly downward from initial bliss to inevitable despair. The bass guitar, which could be described as the lead instrument here, is played an octave higher than usual and, in sync with the dynamics of the singer's argument, tumbles down at key points. At the bridge a trebling bass with slashing guitar chords emphasize the singer's cynicism.

50. Stevens, "An Evening with Brian Wilson."
51. Wexler, quoted in Schott, "Oversouling."
52. White, *The Nearest Faraway Place*, 258.

"I Just Wasn't Made for These Times"

The track is the album's supreme statement of alienation—alienation from love, friends, work partners, contemporary culture, and the historical moment. However, Brian's understated vocals keep the song from wallowing in self-pity and despair. Instead, through the lyrics, the pounding drums, the temple blocks, the theremin, and the absence of an intro, Wilson communicates the singer's anxiousness, discomfort, and torment.

Written before the other Beach Boys or Capitol had heard *Pet Sounds*, the track suggests that Wilson anticipated conflicts with his label and band, particularly Love and to a lesser extent Jardine. No one, Wilson sings, will help him realize "new things" or ambitious plans. The song complements "I Know There's an Answer," or more specially, "Hang on to Your Ego," in which the undefined "they" look "peaceful" but are really "uptight" and wasteful of time. As Wilson said, on *Pet Sounds*, the lyrics "emitted feelings from my soul and not the usual 'Beach Boys' kind of approach."[53] Wilson realized, as Emerson wrote, that the enemy of self-trust is conformity and consistency: "With consistency a great soul has simply nothing to do. He may as well concern himself with his shadow on the wall." Wilson risked being misunderstood. "Is it so bad, then, to be misunderstood? Pythagoras was misunderstood, and Socrates, and Jesus . . . and every pure and wise spirit that ever took flesh. To be great is to be misunderstood."[54]

"Pet Sounds"

Originally titled "Run James Run," the penultimate track features a reverbed lead guitar line that snakes and coils to the rhythm of a tambourine, triangle, guiro, and the banging of two Coca-Cola cans. The overall effect is, as Timothy White suggests, that of a lonely late-night drive in a downpour, a "solitary flight . . . crisp and shuddersome."[55] The track reinforces the theme of loneliness, alienation, and quest for home or solace—which the controlling consciousness never finds. Wherever he runs, it seems, his burden or his giant, as Emerson called it, go with him.[56]

---

53. Wilson, *Wouldn't It Be Nice*, HarperCollins, 140.
54. Emerson, "Self-Reliance."
55. White, *The Nearest Faraway Place*, 250–51.
56. Emerson, "Self-Reliance."

Emersonian Individualism and the Quest for Wholeness in *Pet Sounds*

"Caroline No"

With "Caroline No" the album ends on a note of despair. The third masterpiece of *Pet Sounds* begins with what sounds like three taps on clanging castanets and then a single pound on a large upside-down water bottle, a pounding that recurs throughout the song and seemingly sounds a death knell. Brian's vocals enter with a harpsichord and address his lover and the loss of her long hair (an emblem of youthful zest), her old self, and her "happy glow." The melancholy lyrics of innocence lost are sung to a lugubrious rhythm that pushes on with harpsichord, thumping bass, and bluesy flutes and saxophones. The devastated and confused singer mourns the loss of youth with its lightness and optimism, once so energizing in "Wouldn't It Be Nice." "Caroline No" reflects his situation with Marilyn: "we'd lost the innocence of our youth in the heavy seriousness of our lives."[57] At the song's recording, Brian was twenty-four and Marilyn twenty. As the album winds down, Brian or the controlling consciousness is alone, signaled by the absence of vocal harmonies on the track. He ends with a prolonged and painful cry of "no," a mark of dread at what the coming years portend. Revealingly, Asher originally wrote "Caroline, I know," which Wilson changed, perhaps to emphasize his aloneness. Song and album conclude with sounds of a racing train and barking dogs. Is life racing by as quickly as that train? Can all we do is bark for a brief few seconds and deliver "sound and fury signifying nothing"?[58] The song, like much of the album, is obsessed with change, the passing of time, and disintegration.

Curiously, later in 1966, John Lennon met Yoko Ono at an exhibition of her works. Lennon, the story goes, climbed a ladder, peered through a spy class, and saw *YES*. That *YES* contrasting with Wilson's *no* adumbrates two very different directions of the pop music icons, specifically, Lennon and Yoko's optimistic bed-ins for peace in 1969 and Wilson's cynical retreat to his bedroom in the early 1970s.

The Achievement of *Pet Sounds*

Released on May 16, 1966, *Pet Sounds* did not have the commercial success that Wilson had hoped. It peaked briefly at number ten, charted for a mere thirty-nine weeks, and would not "go gold" for decades—disappointing for

---

57. Wilson, *Wouldn't It Be Nice*, HarperCollins, 134.
58. Shakespeare, *Macbeth* V.v.

a Beach Boys album.[59] In early July, concerned with the band's image, Capitol released *Best of the Beach Boys*, on which they showered promotional dollars and which lasted on the charts for seventy-nine weeks, competing with and soaring past *Pet Sounds* in sales.

However, the artistic impact of *Pet Sounds* was immediate and has been long lasting. Paul McCartney said that "*Pet Sounds* was my inspiration for making *Sgt. Pepper's* . . . the big influence," and George Martin said that "Without *Pet Sounds*, *Sgt. Pepper* wouldn't have happened . . . *Pepper* was an attempt to equal *Pet Sounds*."[60] In 1998, Thom Yorke of Radiohead called *Pet Sounds* "an incredibly amazing pop record" and cited its influence on *Ok Computer*.[61] Today, *Pet Sounds* is unquestionably one of the greatest albums of all time, ranking only behind *Sgt. Pepper's* on *Rolling Stone*'s 500 greatest albums of all time.[62]

Pet Sounds represents a bold adventure from an artist at the peak of his powers, one willing to risk commercial success to expand the parameters of pop music and to make a grand statement about life, love, and loss. In this "single-minded pursuit" and in its intense exploration of the self, *Pet Sounds* is a very American work, declaring, as did Emerson, Walt Whitman, and Emily Dickinson, that the self and its preoccupations can be the focus of great art. In its glorious obsession with the self, *Pet Sounds* delivers an always-needed reminder of the importance of the self, but a reminder especially needed in 1966 when Americans were about to be compelled, it seemed, to announce affiliations: hawk or dove, segregationist or integrationist, silent majority member or protester. Wilson affirms, like Emerson, that the individual's allegiance is first to himself or herself and the quest for wholeness, a quest not to be restricted by memberships and affiliations.[63] Through *Pet Sounds*, Wilson reminds us that the self can still be imperial.

---

59. *Pet Sounds* did much better in the UK, peaking at number two.

60. The Beach Boys, *The Pet Sounds Sessions* liner notes, 10.

61. DiMartino, "Give Radiohead Your Computer."

62. "The 500 Greatest Albums of All Time." In 1995, *Mojo* ranked *Pet Sounds* as the greatest album of all time ("The 100 Greatest Albums Ever Made").

63. Emerson warns of such restrictions in "Self-Reliance": "If I know your sect, I anticipate your argument. I hear a preacher announce for his text and topic the expediency of one of the institutions of his church. Do I not know beforehand that not possibly can he say a new and spontaneous word? . . . Well, most men have bound their eyes with one or another handkerchief, and attached themselves to some one of these communities of opinion."

Three

Dire Wave

Brian Wilson's "'Til I Die"

DAVE PERKINS

In 1971, the Beach Boys released their album, *Surf's Up*, which featured Brian Wilson's existential masterpiece "'Til I Die." That same year, but seemingly worlds away, philosopher Martin Heidegger created his important essay "What Are Poets For?" In both works, one can hear the psychological and spiritual distress of modernity. Each work is a cultural artifact of the late 1960s, reverberating with the Cold War's threat of nuclear annihilation and modernity's deteriorating spiritual foundations. In these works, Wilson and Heidegger express modernity's weight, its spiritual, intellectual, and physical stresses. Humankind's fragmentation, its alienation from the earth, the self, and spiritual surety are a shared subtext in both works.

In Heidegger's essay, the modern human condition is depicted as unrooted. It hangs precariously above an abyss and without a foundation to bear its existential weight. In that state, humankind is unshielded and vulnerable, a state of being which, ultimately, becomes psychologically and spiritually caustic. This is "the world's night," says Heidegger. It is destitute and spiritually dark. Brian Wilson has that state of being in mind when he writes, "it kills my soul."

God Only Knows

Brian[1] composed "'Til I Die" not only under the epochal conditions described by Heidegger, but also in the wilderness of his own dark time. The song points toward the forces that drove Brian to withdraw from performance and from the public life he had achieved by way of success in the popular arts. Importantly, however, the song transcends the experience of the composer and achieves universality by voicing the existential fears and anxieties of twentieth-century life. In this chapter, I will put "'Til I Die" into conversation with Heidegger's "What Are Poets For?" and Paul Tillich's *The Courage To Be* and *Theology of Culture,* and attempt to shine light on the weighty questions that constitute the framework of Brian's song. I will attempt to find another perspective from which to view not just Brian's oft-publicized troubles, but what he made of them in this one song that fellow Beach Boy Bruce Johnston referred to as "the last great Brian Wilson song" and "Brian's heaviest song"[2]—the beautiful "'Til I Die," which took root in hope and bloomed in spite of those troubles.

The Myth of Brian

In 1965 the Beatles pushed rock and roll beyond dance music and popular entertainment with their album *Rubber Soul.* In the ensuing expansion of pop music culture, the name Brian Wilson was on a short list of American pop music makers deemed capable of challenging the Beatles' creative supremacy. The Beatles themselves acknowledged the Beach Boys' 1966 album *Pet Sounds* as a giant step forward in rock and roll's evolution toward serious art. *Pet Sounds* pushed the Beatles to reach high in the conception and production of their next album *Sgt. Pepper's Lonely Hearts Club Band,* arguably the standard by which all rock albums are still judged.

By the time *Pet Sounds* was released, Brian, like the Beatles, had retired from touring—ostensibly to focus his genius and time on mastery of the studio arts. The Beatles and Brian Wilson would become something new in pop music, artists who do not perform publically—singers and songwriters whose stage is the recording studio. Brian claimed he was in search of something he could find only in total dedication to the recording studio. However, he was also running away from something that had become burdensome, even frightening to him—life in the spotlight and

---

1. There were three Beach Boys members with the surname Wilson. To avoid confusion, I will refer to Brian Wilson by his first name from this point onward.
2. Leaf, *Beach Boys and the California Myth,* 144.

the pressures of celebrity. Increasingly uncomfortable with travel and the stage and feeling the weight of emotional stress, Brian quit touring with the Beach Boys in 1965. Since then, little has been written about Brian in which his mental health is not explicitly or implicitly an issue. Brian's much-publicized reclusiveness and the psychological conditions behind it became the lens through which his work was interpreted. They remain a major theme in the Brian Wilson myth.

The Brian Wilson myth, which still circulates in pop music culture,[3] was a contributing factor not only in the Beach Boys' commercial survival, but also in critical perception of the group as significant and relevant to the times. The Brian myth sustained the band through cultural shifts and changes in pop music sensibility that, had Brian's star not been secure, would have left the group as little more than pitifully out of fashion. It also kept Brian's reputation on life support through years of creative famine.

The myth's basis was the romanticized tragedy of a wounded hero (genius) coupled with the hope of his restoration. When Brian first retreated from performance and celebrity, no one knew that he was suffering from an actual mental health condition, schizoaffective disorder. Missing that information, Brian's reported drug use and psychological fragility were interpreted as symptoms of the self-indulgence that had become common among entertainers. Brian's name was sometimes associated with dead musical heroes Brian Jones, Mama Cass, Hendrix, Joplin, and Jim Morrison, casualties of rock and roll stardom. However, to have a pop culture genius—something of an innocent at that—living in a socially vegetative state was, in its refusal to go away, more unsettling than death by overindulgence. The death of a rock star produced a shock no matter how extreme her or his patterns of excess and consumption had been. In Brian's case the public watched in slow motion the unfolding of a story whose ending was painfully predictable, or so it seemed.

Reports of Brian's degenerated physical and mental state appeared regularly in the pop music press. The name Brian Wilson took on a notoriety not unlike the genius recluse of the previous generation, Howard Hughes. Brian's story became a cautionary tale. Along with a growing list of pop obituaries, it contributed to the youth generation's sense that they were witnessing the dimming of their stars. Also at stake was that generation's

---

3. Released in June of 2015, the feature film *Love and Mercy: The Life, Love, and Genius of Brian Wilson* is the latest expansion of the myth of Brian.

pride in their young creators. Any naïve sense that the creation of notable art equated with virtue was disappearing.

Early in the 1970s, a generation's luminaries, the constellation of creative artists whose work once appeared of such vitality that it would surely last for decades was breaking apart. Twentieth-century culture industry had not only commodified bad behavior, but also begun the institutionalization of a destructive tendency that exploited entertainers' shortcomings and romanticized the psychological consequences of modernity and celebrity. Self-destruction became a bankable pursuit for rock musicians. Drug use and fast living were glamorous; they sold concert tickets and recordings. In such a cultural free-for-all, Brian's descent into darkness was not of necessity a liability. In fact, it added authenticity to his band's persona. As unintentional as they may have been, Brian's personal problems counterbalanced the Beach Boys' sweet vocal harmonies, non-confrontational lyrics, and dated performance style. As the Beach Boys slipped out of step with trending sensibilities and aesthetics, the romanticizing of Brian's troubles had the unanticipated effect of helping compensate for the aesthetic shortfall of his band.

Brian's contributions to pop music were mythologized by peers and critics not on the basis of sensational and sad stories alone. As a creative force, Brian was worthy of mythologizing. He owned an undeniable musical greatness and was a masterful creator of sonic textures that, while organic and familiar, defied the ear's ability to separate them into their contributing sound sources. As such, Brian's sonic amalgams can be described as celestial tones. They had an inherent spiritual quality and, in partnership with Brian's melodies, seemed connected to something transcendent. Brian's celestial tones imbued lyrics and vocals with colors that added height and weight of meaning. With "'Til I Die," such harmonic choices promoted the perception that the song originated in a higher consciousness, perhaps, even, a deep personal spirituality.

The myth of Brian stays alive in part by the ongoing practice of interpreting Brian's songs by way of his pain and suffering. For some music journalists and listeners, every song since 1966 in which Brian played a compositional role can be reduced to Brian's response to or acting out of his psychological unsteadiness. Whether it is his childlike, naïve qualities or the "old soul," existential burden we feel in "'Til I Die," many of the musical, lyrical, and sonic colors on Brian's palate have been, at one time or another, sourced to his much-discussed mental instability or to the fragile genius that is often believed to be the root of that condition.

Most useful to any mythmaking process is the hero's Homeric return from darkness—even if the homecoming is played out in a transitory rematerialization in one evocative song like "'Til I Die." The hero who survives Hades or the abyss and returns to the land of mortals carrying with him esoteric knowledge is the stuff of legend. The guitar-wielding hero—flawed, cursed, unlucky, wounded and, therefore, credible—was already a familiar pop culture theme by the time Brian tasted success. Many Brian Wilson fans waited expectantly for his return and looked hopefully in post-*Pet Sounds* Beach Boys songs for signs of his reemerging life-force.

Brian has given us a wonderful invitation to look deeply into his work. He has supplied the genius, the perilous journey, and a homecoming, which, in the era of "'Til I Die," began coming piecemeal in occasional Winston Niles Rumfoord-like materializations[4] in songs. But, Brian has also bequeathed us a problem. Other than a few lyrical crumbs and occasional comments in interviews, Brian offers little instructive, guiding information of a deeply theological nature on his experience and endurance of the abyss. Can a truth be gleaned from Brian's work that has a prophetic or priestly quality, one that precipitates a rise in consciousness or calls to the listener for a change in thinking and behavior?

When listening to "'Til I Die," it is easy to conclude that Brian is doing some kind of higher-order business. This is possible in part because we came to expect truth telling from the great artists of Brian's era. We the listeners witnessed and encouraged the elevation of the popular music artist to a leadership role in our intellectual, spiritual, and cultural evolution. In addition, there are the clues scattered down the path of the Beach Boys' repertoire—"God Only Knows," "I Just Wasn't Made for These Times," "When I Grow Up to Be A Man," and others. We suspect that Brian has learned more about "the answer" than he knew in 1966 when, in "I Know There's an Answer," the Beach Boys claimed there was one out there somewhere. But, what is it? And, is he trying to tell us in "'Til I Die"?

Heidegger, Tillich, and Brian

If you consider the beauty of "'Til I Die" and, then, the contradicting conditions of its creation—the song's emergence out of existential anxiety—you

4. See *The Sirens of Titan* by Kurt Vonnegut.

God Only Knows

can appreciate its affinity to the works of Heidegger and Tillich cited above. A shared concern for how humankind can and must overcome the delimiting forces of modern existence connects them. In "'Til I Die," Brian asks questions with deep existential implications that he then leaves unanswered. It is through Heidegger and Tillich's sense of the times that we can hear "'Til I Die" as something more than an autobiographical reflection of a confessional singer-songwriter. As Brian reflected on overwhelming feelings of "smallness" and powerlessness, a universal statement on twentieth-century citizenship took shape.[5] "'Til I Die" gives voice to questions and circumstances particular to Brian. However, his is the voice of "everyman." Heidegger and Tillich offer a number of lenses through which to view "'Til I Die." Two of them are useful here. They are, first, Heidegger and Tillich's understandings of the problems of human being in the twentieth century and, second, their vision of how artists fulfill a critically important service to humanity by courageously addressing those problems.[6]

In an exegesis of Hölderlin's elegy "Bread and Wine," Heidegger took up that poet's still-resounding enquiry, "What are poets for in a destitute time?" Heidegger's interest in language as the "house of being" and his interest in the nature and dynamics of being itself necessitated a response to Hölderlin's intriguing query. "What Are Poets For?" begins by describing the current age as "the time of the world's night."[7] The divine radiance that once animated and enchanted the world is dimming. Heidegger describes this falling darkness as the "default of the gods." Thus, the falling darkness, the destitution of the age is, at its core, a problem with spiritual implications. Although the deities have departed, human beings do not realize they are alone. They do, however, feel the effects of that condition in the form of the malaise of modernity, in anxiety and fear.

---

5. See Brian's comments on the writing of "'Til I Die" in the documentary film *Beautiful Dreamer: Brian Wilson and the Story of "Smile"* (October 2004).

6. As relates to Heidegger: Let the reader notice that I begin, here, to substitute the term artist for poet. In "The Origin of the Work of Art," Heidegger argues that all art is poetry because it is "the letting happen of the advent of the truth of what is" (72). Thus, I take the liberty of switching terms by way of Heidegger's own rationale. Doing so allows me, then, to expand the idea of poet to include songwriters, filmmakers, painters, and dancers, and to direct the question asked by Hölderlin and expanded upon by Heidegger to Brian Wilson and every individual of the modern age who through the alchemy of art seeks his own symbolic healing from the personal psychic and spiritual fragmentation that is the era's great disease. Moreover, as Heidegger proposes, the poet's—the artist's—work seeks not only his or her own healing but also that of the world.

7. Heidegger, "What Are Poets For?," 91.

Dire Wave

The gods once provided the foundation, the ground in which humankind grew the roots that provided existential stability, surety, and strength. In the "destitute time," however, that ground fails to appear beneath us. What remains is the abyss, the place where human beings come face to face with nonbeing. Without the soil in which to strike roots, humanity hangs in the abyss foundationless and, consequently, faithless—except in regard to its own capabilities. Knowing somehow that it cannot save itself, humanity experiences the current age as marked by a disquieting feeling of aloneness. Such aloneness is ironic in its simultaneity with the era's pride of progress and the promise of technological security.[8] Awakening to the feeling of teetering on the edge of nothingness, human beings experience a kind of terror when, for the first time, they glimpse their foundationless reality. Confronted by the abyss, human beings encounter not simply the possibility of their full and final fragmentation, but ultimate meaninglessness and nonbeing. The existential securities that humankind once had—self-invented or not—are gone. We no longer have a sure answer to or reason for our existence and for what now seems to be the empty finality of finitude. This was arguably the existential issue of the era in the essays under consideration here. Similarly, it is the dark energy behind Brian Wilson's "'Til I Die."

Drawing from Rilke, Heidegger says, "The time remains destitute not only because God is dead, but because mortals are hardly aware and capable even of their own mortality. Mortals have not yet come into ownership of their own nature."[9] To come into the understanding and ownership of its own true nature is a requisite for the wholeness of being that is absent in the age of the world's night. It is in regard to this all-important matter that Heidegger imagines a hazardous role for the artist: "In the age of the world's night, the abyss of the world must be experienced and endured. But for this it is necessary that there be those who reach into the abyss,[10] for "only within reach of this site, if anywhere, can traces of the fugitive gods still remain . . ."[11] Among the citizens of an era whose gods have departed, artists forge a link between humanity and divinity.

Heidegger took notice that artists, in pursuit of truth, are often willing to go where others will not go—even into that most fearful place, the abyss.

8. Ibid. 111–17.
9. Ibid, 96–97.
10. Ibid, 92.
11. Ibid, 93.

For some artists, the act of making such a choice is a natural one. While courageous, such acts are not necessarily born out of heroism, although under certain circumstances they can be. Instead, such acts are a natural response for some artists, who, when they see the necessity, will attempt to fashion beauty from ashes. "What Are Poets For?" depicts artists responding creatively to circumstances that delimit. Under such circumstances, their creative acts are capable of producing a light, an illumination, which reveals, among other useful things, something of the nature of human being. The production of illumination is one of the artist's important roles in response to the era's growing darkness. The light produced by the artist's work has a quality more transcendent, more eternal than the light of the age's humanly generated "technological day," which Heidegger contends is a false security.[12] While the illumination produced within and by creative acts is not itself divine radiance, it lights a pathway to the divine.

Artists whose work reveals the truth of being and leads humankind closer to an understanding of its own nature and a discernment of the times are, in Heidegger's thinking, "valid" artists. How, then, does an artist exemplify validity? It is by helping facilitate humankind's "turning."[13] Heidegger suggests that existence in the time of the world's night is not hopeless; there remains the possibility of a "turn" if humankind can find its way to its own true nature. Until that turning, however, the abyss must be "experienced and endured."[14] Further, the abyss must not be experienced and endured blindly, but with existential eyes open—bravely, courageously, intentionally. For this, it is necessary that there be those who purposefully "reach into the abyss."[15] For Hölderlin and Heidegger, this is what artists are for in the time of the world's night—to go where others are unable or unwilling to go.

Why is it necessary that the abyss be not only experienced but also endured? First, it is in living with its unrootedness and in acknowledging that it cannot truly save itself that humankind begins to find the depth of wisdom necessary to understand both its own true nature and the dynamics of being. Moreover, it is there that humankind discovers that the necessary realization of its true nature involves a reconnection to the natural world,

---

12. Ibid. 115–16.
13. Ibid.
14. Ibid, 92.
15. Ibid.

which it has sought to dominate and commodify.[16] To heal its relationship with the earth, humankind must reject the hubris and pride of species that estrange humanity from the natural and spiritual worlds in which it has its being. Endurance of the abyss engenders this humility. It is also in endurance of the abyss that hope is perfected. Hope is the first and sometimes only counter to nonbeing.

As it is a place of terror and destabilization, humans do not often experience the abyss willingly. More often it is in catastrophic circumstances, for instance as a result of great loss or where death comes close. While many individuals sense the nearness of the abyss as they experience the general malaise of the era, for individuals like Brian there can be a more profound encounter. Its profundity lies, in the end, in what the artist makes of it. Brian's encounter of the abyss became endurance as his anxieties drove him to a yet further remove beyond the particular issues that first caused him to withdraw from public view. As those anxieties overtook and overwhelmed him, mere experience of the abyss became endurance. As with Brian, when the veil of self-security is torn and one brushes up against non-being, it is there that the possibility of feeling a kind of fear never before felt exists. Of that encounter, some artists are compelled to make something useful, even beautiful.

The valid artist responds to the destabilizing revelation of unrootedness by creating something in the face of nothingness, by reaching into the abyss and bringing forth life from non-being. Even though most encounters with the abyss are not voluntary, in the experiencing and enduring of the abyss, in living productively in the face of hopelessness and meaninglessness, the artist models one of the essential qualities of human nature the discovery and utilization of which, Heidegger said, would lead to humankind's turning away from the darkness of the age. That quality is courage.

Paul Tillich, whose theological existentialism benefited from Heidegger's early work, prescribed courage in the face of the abyss. The ubiquitous anxiety of the modern age, said Tillich, is not produced solely by being touched by the non-being-ness of the abyss, but in the realization that non-being is a part of one's own being.[17] Non-being belongs to existence itself and must be lived with.[18] If it is not in one way or another endured, anxiety can spiral down into helplessness. While it can be ignored or assuaged

16. Ibid., 113–17.
17. Tillich, *Courage to Be*, 35.
18. Ibid, 39.

though distractions such as drugs, alcohol, or entertainment, the anxiety of a finite being about the threat of nonbeing cannot be eliminated. The fact that nonbeing is a component of true human nature, that it is "finitude expressed as one's own finitude," is the burden we must carry.[19] How, then, to find peace, joy, and hope in existence? How, then, to live productively and with a sense of purpose? Tillich's answer is to live "in spite of"[20] this knowledge. Such an existential posture demands courage—as Tillich referred to it, the courage to be.

In "'Til I Die," Brian Wilson models the courage to be. From within his own endured experience of the abyss, Brian expresses and advocates a kind of faith, a vision and hope of being fully alive despite the existential challenge of finitude. With "'Til I Die," moreover, Brian fulfills his purpose as an artist as it is theorized in "What Are Poets For?" By creating this song while experiencing and enduring the abyss and by singing what Heidegger called a "holy song"[21] in the world's night, Brian achieves the status of valid artist. "'Til I Die" models a way of engaging the questions of modernity in a way that shows the possibility of wholeness in spite of the erosive reality of fragmentation. Despite his shortcomings, and despite his frailty in the face of the abyss, by fulfilling his higher purpose as an artist in destitute times, Brian transcends the superficial status of hit maker, rock star, and celebrity. The term *valid artist* is neither a cultural or music industry classification, but one that identifies an artist as having fulfilled his or her vocation relative to the context of his or her times. In the age of the world's night, it is the valid artist whose work makes a place for the return of divine radiance and illuminates human souls in readiness.

"'Til I Die"

"'Til I Die" is one of the rare compositions in the Beach Boys' catalog where Brian Wilson wrote both lyrics and music. As such, it is arguably the song that best captures the enigmatic Beach Boys leader's philosophical and theological standpoint during a tumultuous period of Brian's life and consequently of the band's history, a time that still attracts investigation and speculation. Somewhere in the interminable process of recording *SMiLE*—the album Brian promised would be his "teenage symphony to God"—it

---

19. Ibid, 35–36.
20. Ibid, 32.
21. Heidegger, "What Are Poets For?," 94.

Dire Wave

became public knowledge that Brian was in a free fall from the heights of satisfaction and critical validation he received for masterminding the American pop classic *Pet Sounds*.[22] Conceived in a moment of contemplation, "'Til I Die" was intended for an earlier post-*Pet Sounds* album but was voted down by Brian's fellow Beach Boys for being too dark. The song finally passed muster with the band and was released in January 1971 on *Surfs Up*. Brian recounts the song's genesis:

> Lately, I'd been depressed and preoccupied with death. . . . Looking out toward the ocean, my mind, as it did almost every hour of every day, worked to explain the inconsistencies that dominated my life; the pain, torment, and confusion and the beautiful music I was able to make. Was there an answer? Did I have no control? Had I ever? Feeling shipwrecked on an existential island, I lost myself in the balance of darkness that stretched beyond the breaking waves to the other side of the earth. The ocean was so incredibly vast, the universe was so large, and suddenly I saw myself in proportion to that, a little pebble of sand, a jellyfish floating on top of the water; traveling with the current I felt dwarfed, temporary. The next day I began writing "'Til I Die," perhaps the most personal song I ever wrote for The Beach Boys. . . . In doing so, I wanted to re-create the swell of emotions that I'd felt at the beach the previous night.[23]

In "'Til I Die," we find Brian standing before, or in the midst of, the great primordial forces that physically, psychologically, and spiritually shape human experience. What Brian seems to seek and what he produces with "'Til I Die" is something akin to the Buddhist-derived principle Kerouac and Ginsburg set loose into American popular culture, "repose beyond fate."[24] A sonic watercolor of existential assurance and peace, "'Til I Die" is an exhale of acceptance, perhaps even relief. Gently, Brian pries back the fingers of fate's hand. With the subverting power of lovely composition and production (spearheaded by Carl Wilson) "'Til I Die" loosens the fearful grip of finitude and nonbeing on its listeners. An instance of creating beauty in the face of, or in spite of, nonbeing, "'Til I Die" models Tillich's prescription for spiritual and psychological well-being—the acceptance of nonbeing as an inextricable component of being itself. Courageously, Brian chooses to create—or, he must create—even though the unstable existential

22. Siegel, "Goodbye Surfing; Brian Wilson's Torturous Effort."
23. Badman, *Beach Boys*, 288.
24. See Jack Kerouac's *On The Road*.

foundation beneath him is shaking him to the core and threatening the collapse of his life's time and purpose.

Brian renders his encounter with the abyss in compositional brushstrokes that are beautiful, even hopeful. This he does without turning away from the fearful, anxious quality of his personal terrors much less the overlaying disquiet of mid-twentieth-century existence. "'Til I Die" is something akin to a snapshot taken during a free fall skydive. It is a moment of repose and clear-sightedness within a blur of internal and external chaos. "'Til I Die," however, did not testify of what one might call a succinct answer to Brian or humankind's problems. Neither did it mark a lasting turn toward health and well-being. In fact, Brian's return to psychological, physical, and social health would be years more in coming.

Brian's momentary clear-sightedness while measuring himself against the forces of the universe may have been helped by a music maker's persistent awareness of the presence of an audience. In the midst of personal and band turmoil, there is at least a part of Brian that continues to hold on to a sense of creative responsibility. It is difficult to imagine Brian not intending "'Til I Die" to have an impact wider than his own emotional well-being, to have a reason for being that surpassed catharsis, self-care, and personal lament.

Brian makes his personal concerns universal concerns in "'Til I Die." When Brian leaves the particulars of his personal trouble unspoken, he leaves available spaces where listeners may sing into the song their own issues, be they particularly personal or expressions of the era's existential trauma. Exercising restraint on spelling out his own fears and issues, Brian opens for the listener room to make a claim of meaning on the song's lyric and to shape its emotional impact. "'Til I Die" provides sounds and musical arrangements that guide the listener emotionally to a deep personal involvement with the song. Brian invites them to hear his questions and concerns as their own.

Still, if "'Til I Die" is a product of Brian's journey into the abyss, if it represents the truth procured in the artist's "reach into the abyss," it does little, on its surface, to bear witness of the pain and suffering involved. Relative to what we know of Brian's journey into darkness and self-imposed exile, the song seems at first listen experientially detached and emotionally soft. Relative to the suffering Brian was experiencing when the song was written, it is within reason to expect his or any song reflecting such experience to have a striking emotional payoff. However, compared to the

Dire Wave

reported depth of Brian's anguish, the lyric is shallow. It is certainly not mythic in scope. "'Til I Die" is not a brightly lit revelation, not a startling prophecy, not a Technicolor vision of how human beings can save themselves from the spiritually corrosive aspects of modern life. On its surface it is merely a confession of helplessness coupled with an acquiescence that that is the way things are and will forever be for Brian, perhaps for us all. He will, until he dies, be no more than the leaf blown by the wind, a little cork on a vast ocean, a pebble in a landslide. It would seem that there is no great truth there. No message or method to preach. No new idea for a generation for whom "the new" was nearly salvific. Just questions—three questions.

Three Questions

Brian constructed the lyric of "'Til I Die" in three four-phrase verses. Each verse opens with a metaphor for self where the writer considers his relationship to the universe, its forces and, ultimately, to nonbeing. Each second phrase serves to illustrate the effects of the chaos of the abyss on the individual. The first and second phrases, working in concert, imagine the writer variously as a little cork floating atop the raging waves of a tumultuous ocean. Secondly, he is a rock dislodged from its secure place on the mountainside and thrown down in a landslide. Finally, he is a detached leaf, torn away from its life source by strong winds. Writing in the first person, Brian captures the impact of personal experience, of seeing his diminutive stature and insignificance in relation to the great forces of the universe. In this, Brian speaks for us all. In the autobiographical and reflective song form, the personal becomes universal. The listener is welcomed into the writer's revelation where the listener can see it as her or his own. The song becomes a reflection on human being, not merely the experience of an individual.

The song's third phrases are its engines of meaning. Each phrase is a question, simple and related directly to the preceding metaphors and the primordial forces acting upon them—raging waves, strong wind, gravity. Brian asks, how deep is the sea? How great a fall is in store? And, how long will the wind blow him about? The singer repeats each question as if to double down on meaning and serve notice of the importance of the questions for the listener. Ostensibly, the questions are fearful. They express Brian's concern with his fate as the reality of his frailty, smallness, and ephemeral nature, i.e., his finitude, breaks like a wave on his consciousness.

In other hands and ears, a much darker musical accompaniment might have followed such questions. The dialectical partnership between the heavily weighted questions and the hopefulness of Brian's harmonic and sonic palate allow the listener to live with the weight of the questions without being crushed. After all, it is fearful enough to ask one's self these questions, much less to assume responsibility for their answers. By creating a beautiful sonic and harmonic setting, Brian bequeaths the song a shelf life it would never have had if its existential subject matter, the dark energy of the abyss, was allowed to reign.

Following rhetorical logic, it would be in each verse's fourth phrase that, in lieu of answering the questions posed in the preceding line, the writer would make the verse pay off by offering to the listener the acquired wisdom gained through his experience or by which he survived the trials that threatened his well-being. Having thus set the stage, it is typically at this point that the songwriter would make his claim of greatness or grace, where he would tell "how he got over,"[25] how he survived and why he should be listened to, respected, perhaps followed. The opportunity could also be used to point the listener to the source of saving grace. Instead, verses one and two end not in sharp positive resolution but in the blunt force of effect—Brian lost his way, the abyss killed his soul, the wind will never subside. And, it is only in the third and final verse that all three questions of how deep, how far, and how long get answered in the statement, "until I die." And, that answer is not the answer we want. It gives us nothing rational that would help construct hope or faith, and it seems too obvious to have deep meaning. The answer is unsatisfying.

As one who, in Hölderlin's and Heidegger's words, validated his poetic calling and gift by "experiencing and enduring," Brian returns from the abyss seemingly empty-handed of advice or warning. He offers no remedy for the frightening effects of modernity's shaky existential foundation. He draws no map nor does he unveil secrets or teach his listeners how they might survive an encounter with the abyss. He is not a preacher, teacher, faith healer, or shaman. He does not posture himself as a sacrificial lamb whose pain makes a way for us to bypass our own pain. In "'Til I Die," Brian trades not only in ultimate concern but also in ultimate reality the conditions that he can do nothing to change. He has experienced and endured

---

25. "How I Got Over" was composed in 1951 by gospel singer Clara Ward. The song has been recorded by a number of artists. It speaks of overcoming great difficulty by way of divine help. It became an anthem of the civil rights movement.

the abyss, but he does not equate survival with victory. At face value, his song is far from a celebratory march. There is nothing to celebrate, nothing that can be changed. If there is no good news to pass along about a subject so troubling to so many, what, then, is the point of writing the song? If there is no answer, no response to the anxiety that follows from modernity's disenchantment, its death of god, its loss of something to believe in, of something that offers meaning in the face of nonbeing, of solace in meaninglessness—if there is no good news, nothing to gladden, nothing more than the "live for today" preached by a number of Brian's contemporaries, if the questions cannot or will not be answered, why bother? Why write a song like "'Til I Die" other than to wail lament?

Says Heidegger, "To be a poet in a destitute time means: to attend, singing, to the trace of the fugitive gods. This is why the poet in the time of the world's night utters the holy. This is why, in Hölderlin's language, the world's night is the holy night."[26] The three questions of "'Til I Die" have no concrete answers that the listener can readily supply. Neither does Brian answer them. However, the asking is necessary and important, both to him and to his listeners. By posing the questions, Brian takes another step toward his validation as an artist who has reached into the abyss and brought out truth of some kind that he can offer as his holy utterance, his song in the world's night—a song that helps trace for his "kindred mortals the way toward the turning."[27]

First, the asking is mechanical. It is the device by which the songwriter invites the listener to consider what is at stake. The fact that neither he nor we can resolve the questions is essential to Brian's commentary on being. There are no answers or solutions to the problem of finitude. Our incapacity to give concrete answers puts us into a position of pondering how we can experience ourselves as fully alive when our answers elude us. We must somehow come to terms with both the immediacy and finality of nonbeing. As Tillich proclaims, courage is our best posture in this matter. Giving voice to questions of being that stir anxiety and illuminating those questions with the revelatory light that evocative music generates is courageous even if the vitality of the act gets dismissed as pop music affectation. The creation of "'Til I Die" is an act of creating and, therefore, being . . . "in-spite-of."[28]

---

26. Heidegger, "What Are Poets For?," 94.
27. Ibid.
28. Tillich, *Courage to Be*, 43.

To whom or to what is Brian addressing his questions? To the listener? To himself? To God? To the universe? Inasmuch as the song both draws from and expresses the nature of being, it relates to all of those. More so than the acts of claiming, proclaiming, or naming, the act of asking represents the existential posture most in balance with powers beyond human understanding and control. The attitude of "'Til I Die" is not that of the upward thrust fist, which became iconic in '60s and '70s pop culture. It is, instead, open hands, palms up, wanting and willing to receive, which is the timeless posture of human resiliency.

In asking the three questions, Brian implicitly suggests a fourth. This question, which makes the three not unnecessary but moot, is, "Does it really matter?" If I am falling from a great enough height to end me, does it really matter how far the fall? If I can drown in ten feet of water, does it matter if it is a mile deep? Why allow the threats of nonbeing to delimit life and the joy of being if nonbeing is inevitable and its measure meaningless? Brian's questions cannot be resolved except in nonbeing, i.e., until death. In the meanwhile, they can only be grappled with and resisted, or somehow lived with, endured. Fullness of being involves finding repose beyond the fate of finitude, which is not simply the final fate, but the ever-present nonbeing pointed to by Brian's questions. This is the nonbeing that Tillich argued was an ever-present component of being. Our hopes for the future exist in tension with our awareness of the nonbeing interwoven in our finite state, and the questions echo without final resolution, as Brian said, until we die.

"'Til I Die" is an example of an artist creating fully out of his or her belief that music can produce divine radiance. It is a creative act in the face of the futility asserted by nonbeing. Going beyond the popular '60s expression "music can save the world," "'Til I Die" represents a claim on the idea that creative acts can alter humankind's relationship to existence itself. The illuminative beauty of "'Til I Die" allows the listener to glimpse a way of being in the world that cannot be fully diminished by existential anxiety. We can face existential anxiety courageously as long as we have holy songs, as long as those who write and sing them lift and carry us through the world's night. We can rejoice in finitude, sing in our chains . . . as long as the music plays. Brian Wilson shows how in three- and four-minute stretches of pop song time that the negating forces that threaten from the fringes of existence are kept at bay and denied victory. If Brian does, in fact, offer an answer to his existential questions, we might see it as the music itself.

Dire Wave

Music can be divinely radiant space in which existential questions resolve in spiritual, emotional, and, what brain scans now suggest, electrochemical fulfillment.

"'Til I Die" is not the musical adaptation of a grand revelation sparked by an encounter with the abyss. Its truth is subtle; the path to find that truth is less clearly marked. In sound and word, harmony and melody, the writing and performance of the song does not as much tell as it models. And, it models not maxims but a way of being fully alive. As did the valid poet described in "What Are Poets For?," Brian reached into the abyss—his own, our own—and brought back to the world in the form of a song not something to preach, but simply, profoundly a place to stand in relation to the primordial powers of the universe. This is what Brian offers, what "'Til I Die" models: a place to stand and a posture for doing so in relation to the unalterable fate of finite being.

The Dire Wave

Just a half-dozen years before "'Til I Die," the Beach Boys exuded youthful verve with the idea that riding a wave is like sitting on top of the world. Because a few years in the world of pop music can equate to a lifetime of experience, good and bad, Brian's contribution to *Surf's Up* does not boast of the physical prowess to dominate nature or even of the joy of simple pastimes. His experience of the abyss has left him not as master of the wave but as a diminutive cork at the sea's mercy. Absent is the lyrical depiction of a young man just coming into his powers who carves the face of the wave—up, down, left, or right at his whim. Instead, storm and current push Brian about. The once-confident voice confesses that he lost his way and, with that, the self he once thought he knew. It has become clear to him that some waves cannot be dominated. Some obstacles are insurmountable or nearly so, and some experiences break the will, they kill the soul.

"'Til I Die" is not the confession of a self-absorbed popular wise man. Nor is it the triumphant bravado of a Jim Morrison-like shaman preaching from the pulpit of his own will to power. The voice of "'Til I Die" is far more humble. It is nuanced with a wisdom regarding which the singer can make no claim of authorship. The song reflects the humility Brian was gleaning from an encounter with the abyss not in his past but, in fact, immediate and ongoing, its intensity brooding behind subtle lyric and lovely sounds. Simultaneously personal and universal, the song's seeming lack of an agenda, its modest un-preachiness reads as maturity and wisdom. Whatever the song's message may be, it seems trustworthy. Even though the song gives no instructions and even if the listener suspects the imminent return of disquiet as the sound fades and the song comes to its end, we sense that the song is offering us something.

To the artist who grapples with questions of being, of meaning and human purpose, Tillich counsels, "No premature solutions should be tried; rather, the human situation in its conflicts should be expressed courageously. If it is expressed, it is already transcended: He who can bear and express guilt shows that he already knows about 'acceptance-in-spite-of.' He who can bear and express meaninglessness shows that he experiences meaning within his desert of meaninglessness."[29] The artist should not respond to the false impulse to conceive answers where none exist. As praiseworthy as "'Til I Die" as a composition might be, it is perhaps more praiseworthy that Brian does not fall prey to that temptation.

The encounter with that which strikes fear and stirs anxiety—the threat of non-being—is the dire wave that Brian senses cannot be conquered. Yet, what Brian seems to be saying in his refusal to turn his experience into a musical object lesson or Sunday school testimony is what his band counseled years before—catch the wave, ride it, and do your best to avoid the wipeout. Try as he might have, Brian, himself, suffered a wipeout while riding the wave of pop stardom. With "'Til I Die," Brian is back in the water practicing buoyancy if only as a cork. He has chosen to respond to his encounter with the abyss by continuing to act creatively. In doing so, he models creative action as spiritual practice. Music is the activity that kept Brian afloat, and connected him to that thing which in song and interview he referred to as God.

Brian's greatness as a music composer and sound sculptor allows him to infuse an existentially anxious lyric with a restfulness and beauty that withstand the spiritual and psychological difficulties of contemporary life by modeling how one can experience and endure the abyss and yet be fully alive, how one can live productively despite a fear-provoking realization of the proximity of nonbeing. The act of creating is perhaps Brian's greatest answer to the existential questions of his time, his exemplification of living fully in spite of fear and anxiety.

As with many great recordings, the composer's musical choices define how we hear and process the song's lyric. Were it not for Brian's

---

29. Tillich, *Theology of Culture*, 75.

compositional and production greatness, which by 1971 had been studied by his brother Carl and brought to bear on *Surf's Up*, "'Til I Die" might be a lament. To whatever extent the song can be heard as a lament, it is not a dirge. It is not funerary; it does not sound like the end of something much less of everything. Nor is it a beginning, some new truth or fresh revelation of how to live well. Its concern is an old one, and it voices that concern musically in an equally ancient manner—like waves lapping on a prehistoric shoreline, eternal yet earthbound in its rhythm. The track taps into one of the earth's primordial rhythms, that of moving water. "'Til I Die" keeps flowing, keeps coming, wave after wave, carrying the listener into an emotional space that is peaceful and hopeful despite the song's refusal to attempt conclusion through the articulation of a convenient truth or by promising an alternate route around existential challenges. Sounding celestial, and yet organically material, the recording establishes a body-spirit dialectic that expresses the ephemeral yet ancient beauty of human finitude.

If, as Brian conjectured, music is the "voice of God," perhaps we should hear "'Til I Die" as a conversation or, better, a duet. We might even profit from going a step further and hear "'Til I Die" as a co-write. The song, indeed, is not a movement in Brian's symphony *to* God, but *with* God. It can be argued as such in that "'Til I Die" offers very little for the systematic intellect; "'Til I Die" works because the writer has left room for the presence of Spirit. In fact, he relies on it. He invokes it—sonically. He builds a harmonic abode for Spirit and, in doing so, attends to one of the central issues posed in "What are Poets For?":

> The turning of the age does not take place by some new god, or the old one renewed, bursting into the world from ambush at some time or other. Where would he turn on his return if men had not first prepared an abode for him? How could there ever be for the god an abode fit for a god, if a divine radiance did not first begin to shine in everything that is?[30]

The song's harmonic, melodic, and sonic qualities make it a vessel for Spirit. Together, they construct a dwelling place. It is a place illuminated with divine radiance and waiting for listeners to enter the sonic cathedral, partake of the sacrament of song, and sing with Brian a holy song in the world's night.

As electronic culture in the twenty-first century increases its bombardment of human beings with aesthetic experience, we can argue that the

---

30. Heidegger, "What Are Poets For?," 92.

"technological day" Heidegger described is brighter than ever. However, its brightness is also its power to obscure. The deep questions of human being still call to us from beneath the glare of culture's glossy surface. As long as the questions remain, songs such as "'Til I Die" remain holy. They continue to function well beyond their season in pop music history as sonic cathedrals in which divine radiance can still be glimpsed, if only at a distance. These songs show divine radiance not in the past as something lost to the world, but ahead in the future. Songs such as "'Til I Die" beckon and draw humankind toward a fuller turning that awaits.

"'Til I Die" begins and ends with unanswered philosophical or, if you will, theological questions. However, because of the song's brilliant melodic and harmonic moves, we feel we know—or, we know that we feel—the song's deeper truth, which, ironically, produces a sense that it is hope heavy. The song's instrumentation and its vocal approach produce a tangible atmosphere of hopefulness—a hope, however, that remains unspecified. The hope to which it implicitly points is not given form or personhood by the writer. Yet, hope rises up out of the dialectical relationship of words and music. Hope is the song's life force, as it is the writer's, whose response to finding himself on the precipice of the abyss is to sing his holy song. "'Til I Die" does not point to an object or person in which to hope, but creates an atmosphere in which a listener, perhaps the artist himself, may live hopefully and find, if only for two minutes and forty-four seconds, repose beyond the fate of nonbeing. To find moments of repose in the cathedral of song: this is a gift to the listener that, even if no other transactions take place, gives this or any song a reason to be.

Four

Searching for the Perfect Wave

The Beach Boys and the Power of Hope

MARY MCDONOUGH

In perfect harmony set against an upbeat tempo, the Beach Boys' song "Catch a Wave" opens with an inspiring declaration: "Catch a wave and you're sittin' on top of the world." Filled with beautiful images coupled with harmonies and upbeat rhythms, the music of the Beach Boys opens our world to a realm of possibilities, to the power of hope—a feeling we experience when we can envision a better path to the future.[1] Yet hope is much more than a mere feeling; it unleashes a powerful emotion capable of influencing our brain chemistry.

I was never particularly interested in the emotion of hope from an academic standpoint until I was a visiting scholar at the Hastings Center, a well-known bioethics think tank in central New York. One day while researching health care reform I stumbled on an article by Dr. Jerome Groopman, an oncologist and professor at Harvard University.[2] In his essay, Groopman argues that new research suggests the emotion of hope may play a major role in healing.

---

1. My definition of "hope" comes from Groopman, *Anatomy of Hope*, xiv.
2. Groopman, "Biology of Hope."

God Only Knows

Since I have an MA in Catholic theology and a PhD in ethics, I knew of the philosophical importance of hope. Throughout history we find abundant literature on the subject. In Greek mythology, hope plays a mysterious role in the story of "Pandora's Box." One version of the myth recounts how humankind had been living in a blissful state until one day when Pandora received a box from Zeus and was told not to open it. Curiosity got the better of her; she opened its contents, thereby releasing evil and misfortunes upon the world. One item, however, remained in the box: hope. For centuries scholars have debated the reason for hope's placement in the box in the first place and why it remained there. The optimistic reading of the myth is that by remaining in the box, hope is given a permanent home, thereby preserving it for the benefit of humans. In Christian theology, hope is valued as an important virtue. St. Thomas Aquinas argued that it, along with faith and charity, is one of the three theological virtues given to us through grace. Hope helps lead us toward God.[3]

While well-versed in philosophical and theological thinking about hope, I had never connected the therapeutic value of hope with scientific research on the role it plays in promoting physical and psychological healing. Similarly, I had never thought of the Beach Boys' music as therapeutic until a close friend told me the following story. Years ago she contracted viral meningitis from her infant daughter. For weeks she felt exhausted, her head throbbing, her body hurting all over. All she could do was lie in bed in a dark room. The only music she could tolerate was by the Beach Boys, which she played over and over because, as she recalled, "It was the only thing that made me feel better." While she was a fan of the Beach Boys she also liked many other bands but it was this specific group that she played again and again.

Why did this particular music with its seemingly simple, perhaps even superficial, lyrics offer some relief from her misery? I decided to find out. As I began to listen intently to songs by the Beach Boys, I realized their music has greater depth than it appears on its surface. With complex, inspired harmonies and lyrics filled with symbols, metaphors, and inspirational themes, the Beach Boys' songs form conduits of hope; a powerful emotion that in itself can serve as an important therapeutic tool.

---

3. Aquinas, *Treatise on the Virtues*, 118–23.

Searching for the Perfect Wave

The Magic of Music

> I can hear music
> Sweet sweet music
>
> ("I Can Hear Music" by the Beach Boys)

Like the emotion of hope, music is universal, existing throughout human history. Archeologists have discovered the remains of flutes made out of bone that are almost 40,000 years old.[4] Many theories exist about why music is so important to humans. One explanation is that music evolved from the singsong chatter that mothers speak to their infants, sometimes called "motherese." Full of distinctive tones and rhythms, motherese may help mothers bond and communicate with their babies, eventually serving as an important aid for learning the necessary skills for speaking.[5]

While questions about the precise evolution of music may never be adequately answered, its ability to stimulate strong emotions has fascinated people for centuries. Over the last decade or so the scientific study of music cognition, the impact music has on our brains, has grown tremendously. With the ability to use neuroimaging and neural case studies, researchers throughout the world study how and why music affects people in such profound ways. Daniel Levitin, the James McGill Professor of Psychology, Behavioral Neuroscience, and Music at McGill University in Montreal, Quebec is uniquely qualified to research the impact music has on our brains. Before he received his doctorate he worked as a record studio session musician and music producer for several rock bands, including Santana and the Grateful Dead. For years he has studied the intense connection between music and people's brains.

In his best-selling book, *This is Your Brain on Music: The Science of a Human Obsession*[6] and in numerous published research studies, Levitin explores how our brains respond to music. It is, he writes, "the story of an exquisite orchestration of brain regions, involving both the oldest and newest parts of the human brain."[7] Music raises levels of activity in more regions of the brain than any other type of stimulus. When our brains listen to music the auditory cortex, which has the ability to perceive and analyze

---

4. Gaidos, "More Than a Feeling," 25.

5. For a good discussion of various theories on the roots of music see Bower, "Birth of the Beat," 18–20.

6. Levitin, *This Is Your Brain on Music*.

7. Ibid., 188.

tones, reacts first. Next, the frontal regions begin to process musical structure and expectations. Then, a network of regions called the mesolimbic system undergoes stimulation. This is the area of the brain that is involved in arousal and pleasure; where the transmission of opioids and the production of dopamine, chemicals involved in feelings of pleasure and reward, take place.[8] The mesolimbic system is also thought to be responsible for the intense emotional response we have to music.

In fact, the expression of emotion is considered to be one of the primary purposes of music and one of the main reasons people are so intensely attracted to it.[9] Several studies have concentrated on the intensity of people's emotional response to music by focusing on what is known as the "chill response," a physical sensation in the spine that people feel when they consciously listen to music. When people listen to music that gives them chills, blood flow increases to areas of the brain that correlate with the pleasure centers. These regions control the production of dopamine. The more intense the chill response, the greater the activity in the pleasure centers of the brain.[10] This response to music makes it a particularly strong therapeutic tool to treat clinical depression. Simply listening to happy, pleasant music, however, can also lead to chemical changes in the brain even if the listener does not feel the chill response, because the more someone likes the music, the better they will feel.[11]

Not only does listening to music actually change the chemistry of the brain, but two major psychological mechanisms occur that enable music to evoke emotions. The first, called emotional contagion, describes a process where a piece of music can actually induce a specific emotion.[12] Research on emotional expression in music reveals that structures of music share similarities to the structures of expressed emotions in humans. People who listen to music, therefore, can pick up the emotional tone of the music much in the same way that we perceive the emotional tone of others while listening to their speech[13] or watching their facial expressions.[14] In other

---

8. Levitin and Tirovolas, "Current Advances," 214–17; Levitin, *This Is Your Brain on Music*, 186–87.
9. Juslin and Sloboda, eds., *Handbook of Music and Emotion*.
10. Levitin and Tirovolas, "Current Advances," 219–21.
11. Koelsch, "Towards a Neural Basis," 131–32.
12. Juslin and Västifäll, "Emotional Responses to Music," 565.
13. Neuman and Strack, "Mood Contagion."
14. Hatfield et al., *Emotional Contagion*, 12.

words, the listener will mimic, internally, the emotional tone of the music. One explanation for why this occurs is that music often contains acoustic patterns similar to those found in emotional speech. Our brains, therefore, once stimulated by these music patterns, cause us to mimic the perceived emotion internally.[15] Rhythm, musical key, and level of pitch all influence what type of emotion is induced. A slow tempo, minor key, and low pitch have been shown to make the listener feel sad.[16]

The second psychological mechanism allowing music to influence our emotions is known as visual imagery. This term describes the process by which visual images imagined by a listener while hearing music induce a particular emotion.[17] For example, a particular rhythm found in a song may remind the listener of the motion of the ocean, thereby causing the listener to visualize waves crashing up against a sea coast. Theories on symbolic development show that the visual imagination develops in young children when they begin to create more and more complex symbols of the external world.[18] Mental images are generally thought to be "internal triggers" of emotions[19] and studies have shown that music is particularly useful for arousing these images.[20]

While instrumental music has the ability to alter our brain chemistry and activate the specific psychological mechanisms that allow music to evoke emotions, the addition of song lyrics can make the emotional response to music even stronger. Much of music is not instrumental but contains lyrics—poetry put to melodies that can convey strong emotions and messages. Stylistically, lyrics differ dramatically from ordinary speech through their use of rhyme, meter, and symbolic language, but they can be equally as powerful. Lyrics can convey political messages uniting people under a common identity, such as a national anthem like "The Star Spangled Banner"; or under a political/social movement through the use of protest songs. Protest songs have a long history in the United States beginning with the Revolutionary War when William Billings took famous hymns and changed their lyrics to express an anti-Britain sentiment.[21] In

---

15. Juslin and Västifäll, "Emotional Responses to Music," 566.
16. Juslin, "Communicating Emotion in Music Performance."
17. Juslin and Västifäll, "Emotional Responses to Music," 566.
18. Ibid.
19. Plutchik, "Emotions and Imagery."
20. Osborne, "The Mapping of Thoughts."
21. Epstein, *Political Folk Music*, 24.

the early twentieth century, union activist Joe Hill wrote many pro-labor songs to motivate laborers and their organizers. Early on in the workers' movement he recognized the power of song lyrics. In a 1914 letter to the Industrial Workers of the World's (IWW) periodical called *Solidarity* he wrote: "A pamphlet, no matter how good, is never read more than once, but a song is learned by heart and repeated over and over."[22]

Song lyrics play an integral part in our everyday lives. They help us commemorate historical events ("The Battle of New Orleans," "The Ballad of Casey Jones"), help us pray ("Amazing Grace," "The Our Father"), express our love for someone ("My Heart Will Go On," "I Will Always Love You"), act as an outlet for grief ("Candle in the Wind," "Gone Too Soon"), and even encourage us to have fun ("Girls Just Want to Have Fun," "[You Gotta] Fight for Your Right [to Party!]"). In fact the emotional connection between lyrics and listeners is so strong that an online music site actually exists called AllMusic[23] where people can choose a specific emotion and a list of albums and songs will be created for them representative of that particular mood.

The strong effect music has on both our brain chemistry and emotions explains why it makes such a good therapeutic tool. Stroke patients can benefit from music therapy. Playing melodies on a piano or drum pad that emits piano sounds helps stroke patients hone damaged motor skills.[24] For years music therapy has been used successfully to treat autism. Studies have shown that children with autism have less brain activity than other children when observing emotional faces. Music therapy helps patients process and identify emotions. When listening to patterns of music autistic children learn to identify emotions by associating fast, loud rhythms with happiness, and slow, soft ones with sadness.[25]

Music therapy can also help people with dementia. Often Alzheimer's patients can remember song lyrics long after they have forgotten the names and faces of the people closest to them. Petr Janata, a cognitive neuroscientist at University of California, Davis's Center for Mind and Brain, believes that the medial prefrontal cortex is the area of the brain that serves as a hub for emotions, memory, and music. This area of the brain lights up when

---

22. Ibid.
23. http://www.allmusic.com/.
24. Altenmüller et al., "Neural Reorganization," 395–405.
25. Gaidos, "More Than a Feeling," 28.

songs bring up specific, personal memories for listeners.[26] This same area of the brain is one of the last to atrophy as Alzheimer's disease progresses, which may explain why dementia patients have the ability to recall songs. Janata believes that playing music can improve the patient's life by elevating their mood and alertness.[27]

Not only do dementia patients enjoy the music, thereby raising their emotional state, music's ability to stimulate the memory region of the brain has proven to be particularly helpful. In an interview for PBS, Concetta Tomaino, Executive Director and Co-Founder of the Institute for Music and Neurologic Function, summarized the benefits of music therapy for dementia patients: "we can stimulate the timing mechanisms, we can stimulate word finding ability, we can stimulate recognition memory, and even short-term memory function through using music in a specific way that makes available to these patients function in the brain that's still there but maybe they can't get at independently because of the inhibition that has taken place due to their brain injury."[28]

Finally, listening to music may reduce one's ability to perceive pain. A growing number of doctors have begun to use music in clinical situations for pain management. Scientists at the University of Utah measured brain activity and pupil dilation in a test group experiencing pain. The researchers found that the more the research subjects focused on music the less pain they felt.[29] A Swedish study concluded that children who listened to music following surgery needed less morphine for pain control than children who did not listen to music.[30]

The Power of Hope

Wake the world with a brand new morning

("Wake the World" by the Beach Boys)

While it is clear that music is therapeutic and that melodies and lyrics can have profound affects on our emotions, many researchers have wondered if a specific emotion can play a particularly important role in therapy. The

26. Janata, "The Neural Architecture," 2579–94.
27. Beck, "A Key for Unlocking Memories," D2.
28. Tomaino, "Music Therapy for Neurological Conditions."
29. Bradshaw et al., "Individual Differences," 1262–73.
30. Nilsson et al., "School-Aged Children's Experiences," 1184–90.

answer appears to be yes. In 2004, Jerome Groopman, an oncologist and professor at Harvard University, wrote a book called *The Anatomy of Hope: How People Prevail in the Face of Illness,* in which he argues that the emotion of hope has a powerful role in healing.[31] Groopman admits that for years he was skeptical about the role emotions might play in illness because of outrageous claims made by the burgeoning alternative medicine community that people could actually cure their illnesses through their emotions—by thinking positively.[32] Noting the lack of any evidence proving this notion and the fact that such a proposal actually harms patients because it has the horrible consequence of blaming the patient for her/his illness, Groopman dismissed the idea entirely.

At one point in his career, however, he began to wonder about the relationship of emotions and the physical body. For years the scientific community has acknowledged that emotions have an impact on our brains. The field of affective neuroscience studies the neural mechanisms of emotions and has concluded that certain emotions cause specific biological reactions in humans. When people experience intense fear, for example, messages are transmitted through nerve pathways causing a series of hormones and proteins to react resulting in an increase of blood pressure, heart rate, alertness, and the secretion of certain hormones that prepare the individual to either fight the perceived threat or to run away from it. This biological reaction is known as the "fight or flight response."[33] Groopman began to wonder: since we know for certain that a biology of fear exists, could there also be a biology of hope? In other words, can an emotion like hope change the physiology of the body? Can the expectation of a positive future outcome actually help bring about that outcome?

Groopman decided that the best way to answer that question was by studying what is known as the placebo effect because belief and expectation, two critical components of hope, are also key elements to the biological effects of placebos. The term *placebo* is derived from the Latin word *placēbō* meaning "I shall please." It originated in the Roman Catholic Vespers of the Office for the Dead when, during the Middle Ages, mourners often chanted Psalm 116:9: "I shall please the dead in the land of the living." In order to make sure a sufficient number of mourners would attend a funeral, people were actually hired to participate in the Vespers. These

---

31. Groopman, *The Anatomy of Hope.*
32. Groopman, "The Biology of Hope," 56.
33. Brantley, *Calming Your Anxious Mind,* 35.

fake mourners' display of grief was seen as artificial. Hence, people called them "placebos."[34]

Later on the term took on a new meaning, one associated with medicine and the use of a pill with no pharmaceutical value. Doctors would prescribe a "medicine" like a sugar pill that had no medical benefit whatsoever, for their patients who demanded or begged for some kind of treatment. Eventually clinical drug trials began to use placebos in order to conduct medical treatment studies where one group of patients, the control group, would receive a placebo and the other group would receive the actual drug being studied for its effectiveness. The control group would serve as a baseline for comparing the effectiveness of the drug being tested.

However, scientists began to notice an interesting phenomenon. Placebos appeared to have a significant biological effect on people. Then, during the 1970s, scientists began to understand why when they discovered the presence of substances in our brains, called endorphins, which are chemically similar to opiates such as morphine. Subsequent research on endorphins led to the following conclusions. First, there is a flip side to the placebo effect called the nocebo effect. This occurs when a patient is told about potential negative side effects of a drug treatment and is given the placebo pill. Researchers discovered that often the patients will then experience the negative side effect even though they received placebos. Negative suggestions, therefore, can also affect the body's physiology.[35]

Second, scientists learned that the mere suggestion that a drug will produce relief can trigger the production of endorphins that make the patient feel better. Groopman argues that the placebo effect is evidence that hope, indeed, has its own biology. Groopman differentiates between hope and optimism, the latter being an attitude that "things will turn out for the best."[36] Hope, however, is rooted in reality when people can see "a path to a better future" while acknowledging any possible roadblocks that might come up along the way.[37]

Over the last ten years or so, researchers have refined what they know about the placebo response. For example, studies have shown that larger pills, more pills, and even injections produce a stronger placebo effect.[38] To-

---

34. Specter, "The Power of Nothing," 31.
35. Ibid., 32.
36. Groopman, *The Anatomy of Hope*, xiv.
37. Ibid.
38. Specter, "The Power of Nothing," 33.

day, placebos, once associated with deceit and bad medicine, have a place, albeit it limited in scope, within the practice of medicine. In 2011, Harvard University even opened an institute dedicated to the study of placebos called the Program in Placebo Studies and the Therapeutic Encounter, based out of Beth Israel Deaconess Medical Center.

Placebos are particularly effective at treating pain and clinical depression. Jon-Kar Zubieta, a psychiatrist and researcher at the University of Michigan, and Christian Stohler, a dentist and researcher at the University of Maryland, are part of a team that discovered how placebos work. In a study published in 2005, Zubieta and Stohler treated several research subjects who experienced pain induced by an intravenous solution. Some subjects received placebos while others were given analgesics for their pain. The group given placebos felt pain relief which corresponded with the release of endorphins in their brains.[39] Stohler summed up the study this way: "The administration of the placebo was associated with the activation of the release of endogenous opioids in a number of brain regions. These results indicate that the placebo response, in other words hopes and expectations, use the same chemical pathways in the brain as chemically active analgesics to reduce pain, improve health and feeling of well-being."[40]

Numerous studies have confirmed Zubieta's and Stohler's conclusions. A 2009 study, showing that spinal cord pain was substantially reduced under placebo, concluded that psychological factors, such as hope, can alter the earliest stages of pain processing in the central nervous system.[41] In yet another study, where research participants experienced brief pain from lasers, the group given the placebo analgesic reported having a significant reduction in the amount of pain they experienced.[42]

Placebos are also very effective for the treatment of depression. A 2011 meta-analysis of ninety-six randomized placebo-controlled trials showed large placebo responses by research subjects with depression. Up to 30 percent of the patients receiving placebo pills responded to treatment, compared with 50 percent of those receiving the actual prescription drug. Thus, the study concluded, the placebo response accounted for up to 75 percent of the positive effects of antidepressant medication.[43]

39. Zubieta et al., "Placebo Effects Mediated," 7754–62.
40. Society for Neuroscience, "Feelings of Hope."
41. Eippert et al., "Direct Evidence," 404.
42. Watson et al., "Placebo Conditioning," 24–30.
43. Mora et al., "Lessons Learned," 1879–88.

Searching for the Perfect Wave

The Hopeful Harmonies and Lyrics of the Beach Boys

Gotta keep those lovin' good vibrations

("Good Vibrations" by the Beach Boys)

Given music's ability to influence our emotions and the powerful effect hope can have in healing, could the music of the Beach Boys be particularly therapeutic? While many of the band's hits are written in major keys with happy melodies, elements that scientists believe boost people's moods, plenty of other popular musicians also include these elements. What, if anything, separates the Beach Boys' songs from those of other singing groups? The answer is their uplifting harmonies and lyrical content containing specific symbols and metaphors. When experienced holistically—through our minds, our imaginations, and our hearts—these sounds, images, lyrics, and rhythms speak to us of hope.

I cannot discuss the music of the Beach Boys without singling out Brian Wilson, the creative force behind the band. Brian, the oldest of the three Wilson brothers, was the chief songwriter, music arranger, singer, and bass player for the group. A big fan of the barbershop quartet harmony style of a 1950s popular vocal band called the Four Freshmen, Brian wrote incredible harmonies. Vocal harmonies, where consonant notes are sung at the same time as a main melody, are a musical skill that gives songs depth, complexity, and a beautiful tone. For Brian, harmonies represented moments of sheer transcendence creating "a feeling of love" inside of him.[44]

Aside from his unparalleled ability to create these brilliant harmonies, there are two other facts about Brian that readers should know. First, he has been deaf in his right ear since he was a small child, making his musical abilities all the more remarkable. He claims that his deafness made him a better musician because he had to compensate "by doing well in sound."[45]

Second, Brian has had a mental illness since he was very young, even experiencing a nervous breakdown in his early twenties. Then, around the age of twenty-five, he began hearing voices in his head saying derogatory things. Eventually diagnosed with schizoaffective disorder, Brian has been under psychiatric care for years.[46] I only mention this because I am fascinated by the fact that someone with profound mental illness chooses to

---

44. Carlin, *Catch a Wave*, 22.

45. *The Beach Boys: An American Band?*

46. Wilson discusses his mental illness in depth in the following interview: Cooper, "Brian Wilson."

write so many songs with beautiful harmonies and uplifting lyrics. I wonder if writing his music provided him with some relief from the symptoms of his mental problems. Perhaps in his early years of songwriting, the music was a type of self-medication for him. I have read numerous interviews of Brian but have never found any evidence to support this claim. Regardless, he eventually turned to illegal drugs, which only caused a sharp decline in his already fragile mental condition. Nonetheless, Brian Wilson composed some of the most beautiful harmonies ever written in popular music.

Harmonies not only sound good to the ear but they also symbolize unity, a kind of camaraderie among musical tones. In order to sing vocal harmonies well, one has to have an excellent ear for music pitch and tremendous vocal control. The harmonies of the Beach Boys, with their depth, angelic tones, and symbolic solidarity, exemplify the qualities that make harmonies particularly adept at acting as emotional contagions. The Beach Boys' uniquely identifiable sound, built around putting three- and four-part harmonies against the lead vocal, blends beautiful vocals together with ease to unleash a rich tone that simply pulls us in emotionally with carefree, happy, and hopeful feelings.

Between 1962, when their first album came out, and the end of 1965, the Beach Boys released ten albums, each with multiple hit singles. I choose to discuss songs limited to this time phase because it was a period of relative innocence for the group; before the drugs, psychiatric breakdowns, lawsuits, and estrangements. During the early to mid-sixties, three themes dominated the band's songs: surfing, cars, and good times. In fact, on the first four Beach Boy albums, *Surfin' Safari*, *Surfin' U.S.A.*, *Surfer Girl*, and *Little Deuce Coupe*, eleven songs are about surfing, fifteen are about cars, and almost all of the remaining songs with lyrics (the band wrote several instrumentals) are about fun activities such as dating, falling in love, and even hanging out at a root beer stand ("Chug-a-Lug").

These three themes serve as emotional contagions for hope as well as stimulants for strong visual images that act as a theater of the eye, showing us glimpses of the good times we are having today and the possibility that tomorrow will be even better. Surfing—an activity almost synonymous with the band although only one band member, Dennis Wilson, actually surfed—embodies hope. Surfing brings to mind sunshine and the ocean; searching for that perfect wave that you know is out there somewhere; the incredible, powerful wave that will pick you up on its crest and lift you high over the glistening blue water while carrying you forward, sun beating

Searching for the Perfect Wave

down on your shoulders, seagulls flying overhead; just you and the wave, without a care in the world.

The band's first national hit was a surf song called "Surfin' Safari." Set to an upbeat tempo with Mike Love's falsetto inviting listener's to come on a surfin' safari, the song describes getting up early in the morning, loading up surfboards into a car, and heading to the ocean. When the band hits the chorus, the song really comes to life with a four-part harmony singing, "I gonna take you surfin' with me," and the words "surfin' safari" cleverly blended between the stanzas of lyrics. The song enthusiastically invites the listeners to leave our private lives full of problems, angst, and the unknown, and participate in a fun expedition involving bright blue water and a sunny day.

Building on the surfing theme, the group released hits in 1963 and 1964. "Catch a Wave" claims that if you catch a wave, not only will you "be sitting on top of the world," but tells us that we can learn an important lesson from surfers: if we want to feel better we should leave the ground behind, get out on the water, and have some fun. Hope-filled symbolism continues with "All Summer Long" and "Surfin' U.S.A." The mere title of the song "All Summer Long" invokes images of vacation, relaxation, warmth, and fun. The song uses a litany of symbols we associate with summer such as T-shirts, shorts, sandals, and miniature golf.

"Surfin' U.S.A." begins with the music of Chuck Berry's song "Sweet Little Sixteen" and one of the most inspirational lyrical images in all Beach Boys' music: "if everybody had an ocean." What a beautiful concept—the possibility of having our own ocean, a private piece of paradise with the serene reverberation of waves surrounding us, warm sand against our feet, the sun beating on our skin, and the sound of seagulls overhead.

The second dominant theme in early Beach Boys' hits is cars. Automobiles represent another hopeful visual image because they embody status, power, independence, and freedom. Cars, like ocean waves, move us forward, take us from one place to another; potentially to a better place, whether a literal geographic location or a happier outlook emotionally; and apparently, according to the band, the faster the car, the better.

The group's first car-themed hit was "409." Written about a Chevrolet car model known for its fast, legendary 409-cubic-inch (6.7 L) engine with a choice of single or dual four-barrel carburetors, the 409 was Chevrolet's top regular production engine from 1961 to 1965. The song declares that this car is so fast that "nothing can catch her." In "Little Deuce Coupe" the band sings that if the car had wings it would be able to fly. The song "I Get Around," the band's first number one hit in the US, is about driving around from city to city while owning the fastest car, and therefore receiving the respect of one's peers. "Fun, Fun, Fun," released in 1964, has a different take on cars because it is about a girl who drives her father's T-Bird, short for a Ford-built sports car called a Thunderbird. She "goes cruising just as fast as she can" and is so quick that not even the guys can catch her. She is having nothing but tons of fun because she drives at such a speed that she "makes the Indy 500 look like a Roman chariot race."

The third dominant theme in the Beach Boys' music is good times. These songs shout out excitement about life, about the future and all the potential good times that lie ahead. Notions about fun represent something to look forward to, something to get us through the bad times. One of the band's most famous hits, "California Girls," uses a lovely contrasting verse-chorus form to celebrate women all over the country, with special kudos going to California girls, "*the cutest girls in the world.*" The up-tempo song "Dance, Dance, Dance" is about a guy who, after a long day at school, goes home and turns on his radio because he's got to dance. "Be True to Your School" features the University of Wisconsin's fight song "On Wisconsin," which served as the melody for Hawthorne High School, which several members of the band attended. The song asks us to be loyal to our schools in the same way we would be loyal to a romantic partner.

The love song "Your Summer Dream" is set to a slow, serene melody with a steady beat resembling the rhythm of ocean waves. The lyrics describe an ideal summer day where a guy drives his girlfriend down to the beach. They get out of the car and begin to stroll along the shore while holding hands. The couple can feel the warm, salty ocean air. Then they see a beam of light reflected off of an ocean wave. After listening to the song, you feel like you have had one of the best days of your life. Finally, the tune "Do You Remember" pays tribute to the founders of rock and roll. Set to a classic 1950s boogie woogie-style rock and roll beat, the lyrics call to mind the great, and flamboyantly delightful, founders of rock music— Little Richard, Elvis, Chuck Berry—who, even though "the critics kept a knockin,'" still created rock music.

Music, Hope, and That Perfect Wave

Don't back down

Searching for the Perfect Wave

But show 'em now who's got guts

("Don't Back Down" by the Beach Boys)

Music will continue to inspire and restore us for generations to come. While all forms of music have the potential to be therapeutic, few share the perfect concoction of heavenly harmonies, hopeful lyrics, and upbeat melodies as does the music from the early days of the Beach Boys. Although most of us will never know what it feels like to ride a twenty-foot wave, drive a Chevy 409, or spend an entire summer playing at the beach, it does not matter. The Beach Boys' music makes us feel as if we are on top of that wave, racing through the streets in that car, and dancing on the beach every day between Memorial Day and Labor Day. Their songs, emblems of hope, take us on a journey toward a promising tomorrow. They capture our sensibilities, transforming us into "prisoners of hope,"[47] helping us believe that the sun will come out tomorrow, we will bask in its warmth for a while, and then we will continue our search for that perfect wave.

---

47. Tutu, "Desmond Tutu Interview." Tutu's use of the phrase "prisoner of hope" most likely comes from Zechariah 9:12: "Return to your stronghold, O prisoners of hope."

Five

Surf's Up

A Spirituality of Awakening and Hope in the Beach Boys

WILLIAM WALKER

About the Beach Boys, I do not write as a music or pop culture critic, nor even as a longtime fan of their music. As a millennial, I was not alive when their cultural significance and influence could really be directly felt and appreciated. What I knew of them growing up was little more than could be expected of most people my age. After coming across some of their later work and learning more about their story, however, I came to appreciate their progressive and creative sound as well as the profundity and intrigue of their lyrics.

Over the years, the Beach Boys' music reached a place that some have called enlightened. In what follows, I wish to elaborate on this enlightened stage first by way of contrast with the Beach Boys' earlier surfing-themed music and image—with a look at surfing itself—and secondly by way of analogizing their musical awakening to the work of philosopher William James and his concept of the sick and healthy minded soul. In particular and most powerfully, Brian Wilson and Van Dyke Parks's celebrated ballad "Surf's Up" is thought herein to reflect precisely this mature voice of

Surf's Up

newfound hope.[1] It is an awakening that is born out of a story and struggle to find hope in the face of conflict, despair, shame, and fear.[2] In Brian's own words, it's an awakening and hope born out of love.[3]

Of course, early on, the critical listener might have dismissed the Beach Boys outright as little more than the latest, greatest pop group during a new era of music, or just as one of the first bands to truly exploit California's burgeoning surf culture. And this was indeed the nature of their original moment: catchy, beach-themed pop hits like "Surfin," "Surfin' USA," "Surfer Girl," and "California Girls" that helped to usher in a rock 'n' roll revolution.

Despite their coincidence with the rise in popularity of surf culture around the world during this same period, the Beach Boys were not really associated with the hippie and countercultural movements of the '60s and early '70s.[4] This apparent inconsistency serves to highlight the gap between mainstream, commercialized surf culture on the one hand—which was typified by the Beach Boys—and local or even countercultural varieties of it on the other hand. Moreover, with the exception of Dennis, no one in the band really surfed.[5] They *were* from coastal California, however, and they *did* want to write songs about surfing. So, the name choice nevertheless made good marketing sense.

Notwithstanding this irony, the Beach Boys continued to draw on surfing and beach themes throughout their career. As late as 1974, the release of their album *Endless Summer* shared its name with Bruce Brown's iconic surfing documentary from nearly a decade earlier. One of their latest songs, "Kokomo" (1988), also one of their all-time greatest hits, was vintage Beach Boys pop music.

The band did move beyond the surfing, beach, and summer fun themes in their songs—and this transition marked a critical transformation in their music—but they never abandoned these themes altogether. They merely transcended them, most fully in the song "Surf's Up," which betrays this very transcendence in the double entendre of the title itself. Furthermore,

---

1. Leaf, *Beautiful Dreamer*.

2. More specifically, as Jim Miller wrote, the stage of conflict that Wilson was experiencing "vented [his] obsession with isolation cataloging a forlorn quest for security. The whole enterprise, which smacked of song cycle pretensions, was streaked with regret and romantic languor" ("The Beach Boys," 195).

3. Leaf, *Beautiful Dreamer*.

4. Though some songs from *Good Vibrations* and *Pet Sounds* did become Bohemian anthems for a time (Guinn, *Manson*, 130).

5. Ward, *A Nostalgic—But Bumpy—Journey with the Beach Boys*.

even though Brian and Dennis both later reportedly resented the surfing image they had come to acquire, there is no denying that the Beach Boys had what many would now recognize as a "beach" or "surf" sound—and partly because they *created* this sound.[6] Surfing and surf culture remain major motifs and associations with the group's name and their music.[7] It will be helpful, therefore, to briefly expound upon the nature of this surf culture, with respect to both its promises and its limits as a social, cultural and quasi-religious phenomenon. In doing so, it should become evident that at a deeper level, rather than misrepresenting "real" surf culture, the Beach Boys initially epitomized much of it—even if inadvertently. It is just that they came to outgrow it.

Surfing Time as Sabbath: Promises and Limitations

> We have constructed an environment in which we live a uniform, univocal secular time, which we try to measure and control in order to get things done. This "time frame" deserves, perhaps more than any other facet of modernity, Weber's famous description of a "stahlhartes Gehäuse" (iron cage).—Charles Taylor, *A Secular Age*[8]

The activity of surfing, about which the Beach Boys mostly knew little, is an art form and technical skill with a steep learning curve, at one level. At another level, it is the height of corporeal and natural experience. It is a most thorough immersion in the physical world. It has the potential to bring people down from the clouds, as it were, putting life's trivialities into perspective and quieting the anxieties of daily busyness. Implicit to "surfing time" is the attitude that privileges leisure over the obsession with productivity that Taylor underscores above.

It is true that surf culture has its competitive, exclusive, and highly individualistic expressions. It can also become a very territorial and hierarchical sport, and one that in some ways even manifests class struggle.[9] The emergence of surfer gangs has not been uncommon, and surfers themselves

---

6. Kent, *The Dark Stuff*, 31.

7. "[I]t was Brian who merged the two almost conflicting genres to create a unique sound that, as musician and fan, Billy Corgan of the Smashing Pumpkins, would point out thirty years later, 'didn't just eulogize cars, girls and surf, but sounded like cars, girls and surf'" (O'Hagan, "A Boy's Own Story").

8. Taylor, *A Secular Age*, 57.

9. Maples, "Surf culture."

Surf's Up

until somewhat recently were very much a marginalized group in American society, getting labeled as "lazy bums" or as "trash." For most people today though, surfing does promise leisure, and for some, it is even Sabbath.[10]

The practice of Sabbath of course stems from the Jewish faith tradition, and constitutes one of the laws comprising the Ten Commandments. Those who keep Sabbath, it is hoped, may discover that they are less driven, less coerced, less hurried. They might find themselves free to *be*, rather than merely to *do*. Surfing, perhaps more than many other leisure activities, really can be experienced as Sabbath. It is not a busy undertaking; it cannot be rushed. Surfing requires waiting and patience. The majority of a surfer's time during an outing is not actually spent surfing, but floating, sitting, anticipating, paddling, and choosing to ride imperfect waves. A surfer is immediately aware that he or she depends on the ocean and is at the mercy of what the swells and tidal currents are doing.

In this way, the idea of Sabbath conceivably corresponds quite closely to that for which surf culture "spirituality" is striving. Abraham Joshua Heschel has said that "The Sabbath . . . is a profound conscious harmony of man and the world, a sympathy for all things and a participation in the spirit that unites what is below and what is above. All that is divine in the world is brought into union with God."[11]

At its best, then, surfing is a peaceful rush of Sabbath. At the same time, the kind of union Heschel describes is difficult to truly experience and sustain. Surfers are also *chasing* the ecstatic. Every surfer longs for the feeling of a wave's propulsion and force underneath him or her upon descent. The looming hope for a ride in which the self gets lost never subsides. It is a drive that keeps surfers out for hours and days on end. In other words, while surfing is therapeutic and leisurely, beneath the surface it can also become ceaselessly frenetic.

In addition to the charge of escapism, surf culture has also been accused of celebrating and enabling a "junkie culture." It seems to be an especially addictive hobby with the potential to consume a person's whole

---

10. According to Walter Brueggemann, "Sabbath is not simply a pause. It is an occasion for reimagining all of social life away from coercion and competition to compassionate solidarity." For Brueggemann, though, Sabbath is also much more than rest and reimagination. It is resistance, and in this respect can indeed be taken as a critique of Taylor's "secular time": "At the taproot of this divine commitment to relationship (covenant) rather than commodity (bricks) is the capacity and willingness of this God to rest" (*Sabbath as Resistance*, 6).

11. Heschel, *The Sabbath*, 31.

existence. This is often how surf subculture proliferates, almost through an experience of conversion and subsequent devotion.

Of course, this sort of culture is not unique to surfing. Other extreme sports have underground worlds and languages akin to that of surfing. Nevertheless, these others, like skateboarding, snowboarding, or wakeboarding, for example, each have their origin in surfing. It is justifiable therefore to speak of the "spirit" of surfing, and it is reasonable to expect that people will have some idea of what that spirit is. Pardoning the cliché, surfing tends to become much more than a hobby. Culturally, surfing has always had a particular lifestyle connotation to it. The spirit of surfing permeates the surfer's whole existence, and in this respect, has a deeply religious aura.

These sorts of underground cultures, however—while they do offer a sustained critique of some of modernity's economism and scientism[12]—can become romanticized, and tend to lack a substantive narrative and organizing identity beyond their respective affinities. For this reason, I submit, surfing and surf culture by themselves do not tend to put forward a genuine alternative or challenge to what Taylor calls "secular time." Moreover, there is a distinction between the anxiety of daily existence, which is fairly easily suppressed, avoided, or ignored, and the anxiety of existence as such. Concerning these two different kinds of anxiety, Christian Wiman notes that "the former [only] fritters us into dithering, distracted creatures. The latter attests to—and, if attended to, discloses—our souls."[13] Even in its vague association with values like peace, tolerance, and harmony, and its pursuit of ecstasy or union with ultimate reality—surf culture is thin in terms of historical content. It lacks both the breadth and the depth to be considered a sustained, living tradition or to form what might be regarded as its own community liturgy.[14]

Furthermore, surfing, like any branded experience, is always at risk of becoming a drug that consumes or numbs rather than deeply fulfills. In limited but significant respects, surfing encourages the life that pop culture also presents to people: bliss in the now. If pop culture entices people to get high, drink more, and lose oneself in the moment, in the night, with this other attractive person—on the dance floor, in the club,

---

12. See Cobb, *The Earthist Challenge to Economism*.

13. Wiman, *My Bright Abyss*, 94.

14. There are those who could challenge this by pointing out that some surf groups have ritualized their spirituality and even produced liturgies of their own (Serong, "There is a god, and she wants us to surf").

in the bedroom—then surf culture likewise invites people to chill out, live it up, indulge, escape, and not to worry about tomorrow. More than singing about it, there is little question that each of the Beach Boys lived and breathed the pop culture lifestyle off and on in one way or another over the course of their careers.[15] It is in this sense that the Beach Boys inadvertently epitomized the stereotype of California in the 1960s and of surf culture in particular.

As Sean O'Hagan chronicled it, "Collectively, those [surfing] songs defined a particular kind of American mythology."[16] Wilson's collaborator Van Dyke Parks testified that "Brian's songs personified the Californian sense of place that all Americans used as their dream escape."[17] As such, especially on the American scene, surfing risks reduction to a religious commodity. It can be celebrated and embraced in the midst of a political economy that in fact runs counter to its spirit without any tension at all.[18] As with anything else then, the market and advertisement industry can take the alternative and potentially subversive force of surf and beach culture and absorb its critique, turn it around, and sell it back to the society that came up with it. Just like that, while it doesn't *have to* happen this way, surfing gets transformed into a consumer good or sedative like any other.

To put it in Kierkegaardian terms, surfing can devolve into little more than the quintessence of "esthetic" existence. For Kierkegaard, "Under the esthetic sky, everything is buoyant, beautiful, transient!"[19] But then, "when ethics arrives on the scene, everything becomes harsh, angular and infinitely boring."[20] Elsewhere, Kierkegaard explains that "the esthetic sphere is the sphere of immediacy, [while] the ethical [is] the sphere of requirement (and this requirement is so infinite that the individual always goes bankrupt)."[21]

As was implied above, surfing does for some connote certain values that are perhaps resonate with hippie culture and the like. At bottom, however, surfing as a pastime, and surfing culture as a social phenomenon, is absent of an ethical core, that is, of the sphere of requirement about which

15. O'Hagan, "A Boy's Own Story."

16. Ibid.

17. Ibid.

18. Bell, *Economy of Desire*, 24. "At its most general level, neoliberal capitalism is about the complete marketization of life."

19. Kierkegaard, *Either/Or*, 367.

20. Ibid.

21. Kierkegaard, *The Stages on Life's Way*, 476.

Kierkegaard writes. Surfing cannot save human beings, in other words, from the anxiety of existence, ambiguity, or suffering that we all seek to avoid, anaesthetize, or pass through. Moreover, to identify with surfing absolutely, as its culture invites, is to confuse the object of surfing for an idea that's attached to it, that it promises, and one on which it never fully delivers.

A comparable lesson can be gleaned from the Beach Boys song "Little Deuce Coupe" (1963). It's a song about a hot rod, and it is as if it is intended to provoke envy: "You don't know what I got!" The important point is not that the "little deuce coupe" brings some kind of deep satisfaction—quite the opposite, in fact. Rather, it is the desire for what one does not have but imagines the other enjoying, that drives desire in this case. Sometimes it is a car. When it is obtained, the object itself disappoints. With surfing, the force of the object is similar, only instead of a being a *physical* object, people want the high of the wave. With surf *culture*, the desire may be more for the *image* of the chill surfer, or the experience of the sensationalized beach life that supplies the veneer of peace and "coolness." In the case of the latter, the enjoyment sought is only based on what *appears* to be obtainable. The object is fetishized. This has been described as the "impossibility of *jouissance*—an enjoyment beyond enjoyment that belongs solely to the other, and which disrupts its recipient's lesser satisfactions."[22] It is an enjoyment that never comes and therefore that furnishes the dissatisfaction necessary for the possibility of a transformation of desire itself.

Melancholy and Conflict

Inevitably, the Beach Boys' music, or at least Brian Wilson himself, runs out of interest in this sort of thing. Surf time is up for him. At a minimum, Wilson certainly tires of singing about it. It may be that Wilson discovers the truth about un-obtained as well as *obtained* objects of desire, namely, that there is a deficiency of gratification whether the object is obtained or not. It could be that he comes to an awareness not just of the loss of any particular desired object, but of loss *itself* as a life force, and as a drive. Slavoj Žižek describes this difference between the loss of an object, and loss per se, thusly:

---

22. Manon, "The Jouissance of Jargon."

Surf's Up

Although, in both cases, the link between object and loss is crucial, in the case of the *objet a* as the object of desire, we have an object which was originally lost, which coincides with its own loss, which emerges as lost, while, in the case of the *objet a* as the object of drive, the "object" is directly the loss itself—in the shift from desire to drive, we pass from the lost object to loss itself as an object. That is to say, the weird movement called "drive" is not driven by the "impossible" quest for the lost object; it is a push to directly enact the "loss"—the gap, cut, distance, itself.[23]

It seems the Brian Wilson and the Beach Boys knew what it was to experience this lack of substance and deliverance. For this reason, their music took a turn into a much less carefree, fun-loving direction. Some have argued, however, that this was their musical and lyrical trajectory all along.[24] There was self-pity and wishful thinking evinced in songs like "Wouldn't It be Nice" or "I Just Wasn't Made for These Times." "I Just Wasn't Made for These Times" and "The Warmth of the Sun" are both wrought with melancholy and composed around the time of John F. Kennedy's assassination. There is lament and great loss felt, as well as yearning for a happier, more innocent time. With "The Warmth of the Sun" in particular, it was not only the words but the chord progression—from C to E minor, to A flat—that was so novel at the time.

With a history of abuse, things always seemed tense between the Wilson brothers and their father, who worked with them as the band manager—especially for Brian, since he was the oldest and the producer. This troubled relationship ultimately resulted in a falling out, and was only one of many trying dimensions in the lives of the Beach Boys. Drugs and descent into indulgences of many kinds for different periods of time were commonplace episodes. Affairs, divorces, and rivalries (and later on, lawsuits) between the band members almost seemed to keep pace with the rise and fall of record sales. Wilson's own decline into depression, drug abuse, reclusiveness, and obesity is well documented.

Brian Wilson also became obsessed with competing with the Beatles. Brian was very self-conscious about what appeared to be the Beach Boys' less hip, less sophisticated reputation in comparison. This led to some of their most cutting-edge and critically acclaimed work, but also the beginning of their decline in popularity. Starting with the renowned album *Pet*

---

23. Žižek, *The Parallax View*, 26.
24. See Sanchez, *The Beach Boys' Smile*.

Sounds, which followed the more popular but still edgy *Good Vibrations,* the Beach Boys all but abandoned their former image and sound. Led by Brian's genius, this shift was also a big risk, and the other band members knew it. Consequently, the feuding and turbulence continued. Emotions and experiences of estrangement, regret, discord, weariness, and wounded pride were plain, routine, and on display in their work.

In *Varieties of Religious Experience,* William James famously depicts and contrasts two religious states, consciousnesses or personalities—that of the "healthy-minded soul" on the one hand, and the "sick soul" on the other. It is the latter, I suggest, that appears to capture the essence of the Beach Boys' conflictual and melancholic stage in their musical as well as personal journey. In the first place, James describes the self of the "healthy-minded":

> In the religion of the once-born the world is a sort of rectilinear or one-storied affair, whose accounts are kept in one denomination, whose parts have just the values which naturally they appear to have, and of which a simple algebraic sum of pluses and minuses will give the total worth. Happiness and religious peace consist in living on the plus side of the account.[25]

The healthy-minded individual, for James, is not one who has worked for or been delivered into said healthy-mindedness. Hence, James also calls these folks the "once-born." Instead, such people by some kind of innate disposition simply refuse negativity and unhappiness when it shows itself, as if it were sheer evil. The healthy-minded cling to their sense of life's beauty and goodness against all contrary evidence. They radiate cheer, enthusiasm, and ingenuousness. At the same time, these persons are prone to blindness about the darker truths of life and the weight of the world.[26] They enjoy an unshakeable innocence and simplicity. On this view, there is a sense in which the conventional notion of surfer culture itself is the archetypal illustration of healthy-mindedness. It also personifies the Beach Boys' early, fun-loving music and reputation. By comparison, and juxtaposed to this, James depicts the "sick soul":

> In the religion of the twice-born, on the other hand, the world is a double-storied mystery. Peace cannot be reached by the simple addition of pluses and elimination of minuses from life. Natural good is not simply insufficient in amount and transient; there lurks a falsity in its very being. Cancelled as it all is by death if not

25. James, *Varieties of Religious Experience.*
26. See Taylor, *The Theological and the Political.*

> by earlier enemies, it gives no final balance, and can never be the thing intended for our lasting worship. It keeps us from our real good, rather; and renunciation and despair of it are our first step in the direction of the truth. There are two lives, the natural and the spiritual, and we must lose the one before we can participate in the other.[27]

Unlike the healthy-minded soul, who only needs to be born once, the sick soul must be twice-born in order to move closer toward the unification of an otherwise-divided self. For James, "The psychological basis of the twice-born character seems to be a certain discordancy or heterogeneity in the native temperament of the subject, an incompletely unified moral and intellectual constitution."[28] Stated differently, the sick soul has an assortment of competing drives, interests, values, and judgments. Such a person bears discontinuity in his or her life. James goes on:

> Now in all of us, however constituted, but to a degree the greater in proportion as we are intense and sensitive and subject to diversified temptations, and to the greatest possible degree if we are decidedly psychopathic, does the normal evolution of character chiefly consist in the straightening out and unifying of the inner self. The higher and the lower feelings, the useful and the erring impulses, begin by being a comparative chaos within us—they must end by forming a stable system of functions in right subordination. Unhappiness is apt to characterize the period of order-making and struggle.[29]

James did finally grant that the healthy-minded religious folks tend to lead happier and more fulfilling lives, but he still insisted that the sick souls are more clearly attuned to the human condition, a condition for him expressed here:

> All natural goods perish. Riches take wings; fame is a breath; love is a cheat; youth and health and pleasure vanish. Can things whose end is always dust and disappointment be the real goods which our souls require? . . . The pride of life and glory of the world will shrivel. It is after all but the standing quarrel of hot youth and hoary eld. Our age has the last word: the purely naturalistic look

---

27. James, *Varieties*.
28. Ibid.
29. Ibid.

at life, however enthusiastically it may begin, is sure to end in sadness.[30]

This dismal sentiment about a materialist outlook on the world is acutely consonant with the prose of "Surf's Up," as will be seen below. James himself early on was suicidal and identified strongly with the existential crisis of a sick soul. His seminal work, *The Will to Believe*, however, testifies to a hopeful emergence—though probably not complete freedom, from such an angst-ridden condition. Brian Wilson's mature music can likewise be recognized as the evidence of a broken but healing artist. What James portrays above is the aftermath of the damage that Brian and others in the band, as well as others who wrote with him, endured.

It is worth noting that this is not a victim narrative, however. The identity and experience of victimhood is something else. Nor does Wilson come across as having suffered through the torment of meaninglessness that existential atheism so fashionable purported around the same time. His is perhaps a simpler and less dramatic, but no less profound, conversion experience of the loss of innocence and a longing for its return. Under the direction of Van Dyke Parks, it is this longing that must have informed and incited the composition of "Surf's Up."

Both Kierkegaard and James sought to diagnose the self, its disarray, and to chart a philosophical psychology of religiosity, though in divergent ways. Their understandings of faith itself, of freedom and of the choice to believe, bear striking resemblance. Neither was rationlistic, but James was the more analytical of the two regarding his elaborate case for faith. It was Kierkegaard, on the other side, who championed the paradoxical, the subjective, the absurd, and the impossible concept of love. So it was for Brian Wilson, as illustrated by his own remarks about "Surf's Up." In 1966, Brian elaborated on much of the song to journalist Jules Siegel in this oft-cited passage:

> It's a man at a concert. All around him there's the audience, playing their roles, dressed up in fancy clothes, looking through opera glasses, but so far away from the drama, from life. Back through the opera glass you see the pit and the pendulum drawn. The music begins to take over. Columnated ruins domino. Empires, ideas, lives, institutions; everything has to fall, tumbling like dominoes. He begins to awaken to the music; sees the pretentiousness of everything. . . . The laughs come hard in Auld Lang Syne. The

---

30. Ibid.

Surf's Up

poor people in the cellar taverns, trying to make themselves happy by singing. Then there's the parties, the drinking, trying to forget the wars, the battles at sea. While at port a do or die. Ships in the harbor, battling it out. A kind of Roman empire thing. A choke of grief. At his own sorrow and the emptiness of his life. because he can't even cry for the suffering in the world, for his own suffering. And then, hope. Surf's up! Come about hard and join the once and often spring you gave. Go back to the kids, to the beach, to childhood. I heard the word of God; Wonderful thing; the joy of enlightenment, of seeing God. And what is it? A children's song! And then there's the song itself; the song of children; the song of the universe rising and falling in wave after wave, the song of God, hiding the love from us, but always letting us find it again, like a mother singing to her children.[31]

Wilson's exposition of "Surf's Up" unexpectedly demonstrates a robust sensitivity to the transience, relative impermanence, and futility of history and human ambition. In what has otherwise generally been interpreted as an individualistic spiritual quest for security in an uncertain and overwhelming world in the Beach Boys' later music, "Surf's Up" narrates the revelation that such security will not be found in the usual places.[32] It takes something more that is both mysterious and available, known and unknown. Kierkegaard calls this different kind of security the religious stage or sphere of existence, in contrast to the "esthetic" or the ethical. Here one meets love and grace: "the religious the sphere of fulfillment, but, please note, not a fulfillment such as when one fills an alms box or a sack of gold, for repentance has specifically created a boundless space, and as a consequence the religious contradiction: simultaneously to be out on 70,000 fathoms of water and yet be joyful."[33]

"Surf's Up" is about an in-breaking and successive awakening to this joy and hope that Kierkegaard describes: simultaneously out on 70,000 fathoms, and yet joyful. In Christian theology, one might speak of it as "Christ's appearance in the world and in our lives—there is no coaxing it, no way to earn it, no way to prepare except to hone your capacity to respond, which is

---

31. Siegel, "Goodbye Surfing, Hello God!"

32. The psychedelic rock groups of the '90s tended to respond to and sing about addressing problems in the world rather than turning inward in the way that Wilson did: DeRogatis, *Milk It!*, 34–35. But in "Surf's Up," the isolated, self-absorbed pattern is arguably broken.

33. Kierkegaard, *The Stages on Life's Way*, 476.

finally, your capacity to experience life, and death."[34] The awakening comes not like a perfect wave, but a most beautiful one; like a wave of love. But it is one that neither takes you away nor brings you all the way in to the shore. There is a walk through the valley first. Only *afterwards* do you find it, or better, get found by it. It takes a second birth, a rediscovery of the innocence and trust of a child. Like James' sick-soul experience, though, the melancholy, conflict, shame, fear, or anger is neither quenched nor avoided. It is braved and endured. You paddle out, ride, and pass through it.

---

34. Wiman, *My Bright Abyss*, 99.

Six

You Need a Mess of Help to Stand Alone

Vulnerability, Judgment, and Love in the Music and Life of Brian Wilson

DAVID ZAHL

A study of the Beach Boys is a study in contradictions. Some of these contradictions are well known, others less so: the band that sung so famously about surfing couldn't "catch a wave" themselves (with one exception). The quintessentially clean-cut American group, for the majority of their career, sported the thickest, most impressive beards the pop world has ever seen. The fun-in-the-sun optimism that belied deep wells of melancholy, the supremely wholesome public image contrasted with a lengthy history of all manner of substance abuse, the assumed solidarity of family ties undermined by decades of lawsuits and ill feeling. The list goes on.

These contradictions—you might call them ironies—are one of the many reasons the Beach Boys remain endlessly fascinating more than fifty years after their first single hit the airwaves. What you see is not what you get. Except for when it is. In fact, the contrasting dynamic goes deeper than the facts of their career. Contradiction was embedded in the songs themselves from the very beginning.

Perhaps *contradiction* is too weak a word. There may be something genuinely, well, cruciform at work.

Religious terminology may seem out of place in describing something so commercial, so pop. And yet Brian Wilson has never shied away from expressing his music-making in spiritual terms. He once went so far as to claim that "Music is God's voice. I've often felt that I was on some musical mission to spread the gospel of love through records."[1] Careful observers know that Brian has not always proven to be the most reliable interpreter of his own work, happy to contradict himself in print and elsewhere. Nonetheless, his words may give us some clue as to how to make sense of the enduring power of the band's oeuvre—and hopefully allow us to appreciate the songs and their creator(s) afresh. To that end, this essay adopts a lens found toward the end of the Apostle Paul's Second Letter to the Corinthians:

> But he said to me, "My grace is sufficient for you, for my power is made perfect in weakness." Therefore I will boast all the more gladly about my weaknesses, so that Christ's power may rest on me. That is why, for Christ's sake, I delight in weaknesses, in insults, in hardships, in persecutions, in difficulties. For when I am weak, then I am strong (2 Cor 12:9).

A Lonely Sea (Full of Tears): Strength in Weakness

"Don't Worry Baby" might be an ideal starting point for such a study, not only because many fans consider it to be the definition of a perfect record (certainly a perfect Beach Boys record), but also because it was originally released as the B side of "I Get Around," in a sense hidden behind the other song. Brian was only twenty-one when it was recorded in early 1964, and yet the promotional strategy resonated with the compromised self-confidence of the lyric, which was written by Roger Christian. This is the song, after all, which opens with the memorable couplet, "Well it's been building up inside of me for, oh, I don't know how long/I don't know why but I keep thinking something's bound to go wrong."

We are getting ahead of ourselves, though. Based on the title alone, and given the *Mad Men*-like context of its composition, one might have safely presumed that "Don't Worry Baby" was written from the perspective of a confident man comforting a hysterical woman. But Brian and Roger

---

1. *SMiLE* liner notes.

You Need a Mess of Help to Stand Alone

flipped that convention on its head, producing a tune about an insecure man recalling all the times his uncommonly demonstrative girlfriend had reassured him.

In what feels like a transparent nod to the powers that be, they frame the next two verses in drag racing terms ("I guess I should've kept my mouth shut when I started to brag about my car"), but it's a testament to the beauty of the opening line and chorus that almost no one remembers it as such. Most cover versions even use an alternate set of words for verses two and three.

The song subverts—probably unconsciously—the rock and roll archetypes of the time. Up until that point, it could be argued that rock and roll was mainly a tough man's game, pre-army Elvis Presley being the most iconic case in point. Early rock and roll was full of chest-beating, focused on generating adolescent male anger, which then was channeled into these great songs. Just listen to the Kinks' first five singles.

Brian, in contrast, opens an emotional floodgate. He was the original heart-on-your-sleeve auteur. Young men had been vulnerable on record before, but usually in the service of garnering swoons rather than expressing actual warts-and-all weakness. Brian's was not the attractive kind of vulnerability; it was the awkward kind. In the song, his girl's devotion even makes him "want to cry." The Beach Boys sang about teenage male tears more than anyone before or since, which may not have scored Brian many dates—but it certainly allowed him to connect with an audience. Rhonda needed to help *him*, not vice versa.

Yet we would be doing both Brian and ourselves a disservice to reduce his innovation merely to the realm of pop fashion and antiquated gender norms. The human aversion to vulnerability is not contextual—some would say it goes back to the garden of Eden, where the shame of exposure caused Adam and Eve to don fig leaves to cover themselves. Their concealment would be the first act of independence from God, the first in a long line of controlled obstacles to intimacy with our creator, a relationship originally characterized by dependence and receptivity. That Brian would refuse to veil his neediness or manage his appearance—out of ineptitude or because it simply didn't occur to him to do so—runs counter to the self-justifying impulse that dominates human history, to say nothing of popular music.

His relative nakedness likely accounts for what would be his greatest theme: the longing for—and astonishment at—love in the midst of weakness that is so beautifully expressed in "Don't Worry Baby." This lack of bluster would certainly make him a hero for those who felt similarly but were afraid to admit it, many of whom would be more than willing to overlook whatever culpability Brian shared in the trials he and his band would face over the years. Underground comic artist and writer Peter Bagge described Brian's appeal in somewhat cynical terms:

> It's Brian's story that so many poor, misunderstood, hyper-sensitive idealists can't get enough of. Not only was Brian the main musical genius behind all those great records, but he's also that most romantic type of Genius: the Idiot Savant, the Tortured Soul. He's become the straight male nerd's Judy Garland.[2]

Thanks to YouTube, performances of "Don't Worry Baby" at the time of its release are readily available for viewing. Gangly and pudgy and balding and clearly nervous, none of the guys—with the possible exception of Dennis—looked remotely like drag racers. Yet from such strange vessels issued such sublime music!

The melody is pure prettiness, and the arrangement full of warmth and ingenuity. Not even the economical echo-heavy guitar solo has dated. The back-up vocals would launch a thousand pop groups. And for a guy who preferred not to use drums in his productions, Brian created one of the most iconic opening drum phrases of all time (by aping, to glorious effect, his beloved "Be My Baby").

Strange vessels would become, in a few short years, broken ones. When Brian quit touring in 1964, bandmate Al Jardine took over lead vocal duties on "Don't Worry Baby." It wasn't until Brian hesitantly rejoined the touring group fifteen years (and several nervous breakdowns) later that he sang the tune in front of people again. In 1981, he took to the mic again, and the results, documented on a well-circulated bootleg and video, are so raw as to be almost unlistenable. The prettiness is gone, and so, for the most part, is the lush backing.

And yet, the juxtaposition of such an immaculate musical creation with its composer's ravaged voice is incredibly moving. There is strength in the weakness, or you might say, the weakness here *is* the strength. The uncalculated vulnerability is what allows the performance to speak on such a visceral level. Furthermore, if we had been taken in by the lyrics back in '64, the 1981 performance reveals them to be what they really are: a heartfelt fantasy bordering on prayer, words of reassurance and unconditional

---

2. Bagge, *Hate*, 18.

You Need a Mess of Help to Stand Alone

encouragement (maybe even absolution) that Brian is dying to hear but cannot convey to himself.

Here, as elsewhere, the song is uncomfortably out of proportion with its vessel, so much so that the presence of God seems like the only possible explanation. But not just any God, rather, a God of grace who bestows his blessing not on the upright, but on the undeserving: "I have come to call not the righteous but sinners" (Mark 2:17).

Lest we romanticize the "wilderness period" Brian experienced from 1967 to 1980 (give or take), the same glaring discrepancy between the man and his gifts was present during the recording of what many consider Brian's crowning achievement, 1966's *Pet Sounds*. In classic Beach Boys fashion, Brian hired a complete stranger to pen the lyrics for that record, having heard a jingle on the radio that caught his ear. Interviewed years later, the lyricist in question, Tony Asher, captured the simultaneous inanity and brilliance that makes Brian Wilson such a rare bird:

> For every four hours we spent writing songs, there would be about forty-eight hours of these dopey conversation about the dumb book he'd just read. Or else he'd go on and on about girls. His feeling about this girl or that girl. It was just embarrassing that he was exhibiting this awful, awful taste. His choice of movies was invariably terrible. TV programs . . . everything. . . . I do believe Brian is a musical genius. Absolutely. Whatever I thought about him personally was almost always overridden by my feelings of awe at what he was creating. I mean he was able to create such extraordinary melodies . . . .[3]

Again, what impressed Asher is how much Brian's art outsized his learning and taste. Some might say the distance represents something of an affront to natural presuppositions about hard work and earning. No doubt contemporary songwriters and producers, those who had sweated for their prowess and experience, harbored some resentment against the teenaged autodidact. But such is the nature of grace. It is unfair. It defies the quid pro quo of effort and deservedness. Not surprisingly, Brian himself has never come close to explaining his talent (or creative process) without resorting to spiritual language.

Naturally, it is tempting to psychoanalyze Brian, and a great many writers have attempted to do so. What was it about him and his background that gave him the courage to be so vulnerable on record? Was it the abuse

---

3. Kent, "The Last Beach Movie Revisited," 25.

he suffered from his father? Was it the drugs he took? Was it simply a matter of mental illness? These are impossible questions to answer—all we can safely say is that from very early in his career, even before the drug use, his capacity for self-censorship was limited.

Indeed, album after album testifies to a diminished mental filter. Brian left in the things most of us would leave out. Who else would have thought it a good idea to include "I'm Bugged at My Old Man" on the otherwise-immaculate *Summer Days (and Summer Nights!!)*? Who else would include detailed directions to his house like Brian did in "Busy Doin' Nothin"? Who else would overtly try to score drugs from a journalist while being recorded for an interview? This isn't to suggest there was anything strategic about his candor; Brian's vulnerability never feels remotely self-conscious. Childlike is how it is often described, and for good reason.

A more mystical writer might theorize that Brian's mental unguardedness contributes directly to his musical inspiration. His internal resistance to the kind of shame and self-criticism that stunts much of our own creativity, for whatever reason, was minimal.

From a 2 Corinthians point of view, Brian's story and music place us in the realm of Martin Luther's "theology of the cross." In his *Heidelberg Disputation* of 1517, Luther maintained that the image of Jesus' death on the cross did not merely reveal the mechanism of salvation but also a fundamental principle about God's presence in the world. He came to believe that God works under the form of opposites (*sub contrario*):

> God receives none but those who are forsaken, restores health to none but those who are sick, gives sight to none but the blind, and life to none but the dead. . . . He has mercy on none but the wretched and gives grace to none but those who are in disgrace.[4]

A "theology of the cross" (*theologia crucis*) in this sense contradicts many of our assumptions about life, to say nothing of the marketplace. According to this scheme, God is not most reliably present in our strengths or successes or the things we like best about ourselves. Rather, God is at work in the world in the place where a person is falling apart, where he is discovering the limits of his power instead of exercising it.

Luther contrasted the theology of the cross with a "theology of glory," which would seek to locate God chiefly in strength and victory. He wisely maintained that the theology of glory tends to be the default of a species

---

4. Luther, *Luther's Works*, vol. 14, 163.

You Need a Mess of Help to Stand Alone

bent on mastery and the avoidance of suffering. In Beach Boys terms, we are talking about the difference between "Don't Back Down" (on which Brian sounds exactly like the kind of guy who *would* back down) and "'Til I Die" (on which confusion and despair serve as the conduits for otherworldly beauty). Lutheran theologian Gerhard Forde phrased the distinction this way:

> The foolishness of God in the cross is wiser than the wisdom of the world. . . . It is not like accomplishing something but like dying and coming to life. It is not like earning something but more like falling in love. . . . The theologian of the cross knows that the love of God creates precisely out of nothing.[5]

The advantage of Brian's willingness to be seen as weak (or his glaring inability to "front" with any conviction) is that he could express gratitude and joy to a similar extent. Some might say that he penned the greatest song about gratitude that's ever been written in the American pop idiom, "God Only Knows"—which also happened to be the first time that the word "God" was used in the title of a song that charted on top 40 radio. And Brian and company were very nervous about that.

Brian elaborated on what was going on when he was writing and recording the song:

> Carl and I kept praying for the highest love to bring to people. We all in the band believe in Jesus and we believe in God and we believe that we were his messengers. So we followed through with our career as his messengers in the world. And that's how we did it. Spirituality is love, right? Love and spirituality are kind of like the same. But spirituality is like ever-lasting love.[6]

The truism that vulnerability is the birthplace of connection echoes the theology of the cross. It contradicts the human intuition that our most impressive accomplishments and proudest attributes are what will win us the admiration of others (and of God). It affirms the reality that to love someone truly is to love them at their worst, not merely at their best. As columnist Tim Kreider once memorably observed in *The New York Times*, "[I]f we want the rewards of being loved we have to submit to the mortifying ordeal of being known."[7] Meaning, we can know someone and not

---

5. Forde, *On Being a Theologian of the Cross*, 105.
6. Fischer, "In Brian Wilson's Room."
7. Kreider, "I Know What You Think of Me."

love them, but we cannot love someone if we do not know them: to know someone fully is to know them in their weakness and shame.

Perhaps it was Brian's preternatural vulnerability that situated him, then, to appreciate the experience of grace in such transcendent and enduring terms, as songs like "She Knows Me Too Well" and, much later, "Love and Mercy" attest. Or take *Pet Sounds*' stunning hymn to "love to the loveless shown," "You Still Believe in Me." The grace of Asher's lyric is underlined by the abundant giftedness of its damaged producer: "I know perfectly well I'm not where I should be. . . . And after all I've done to you, how can it be, You still believe in me." The lover meeting the beloved at his point of (persistent) failure and weakness—his lack of deserving—it is enough to remind the listener of another supremely cracked vessel named Peter, talking to his risen lord over breakfast on, yes, the beach.

Heroes and Villains and the Cost of Weakness

If vulnerability is the birthplace of connection, and love inextricably entangled with weakness, then why do we find it so seldom? That is, why does Brian remain such an exception?

In theological terms, at least Pauline ones, the answer has to do with "the Law," a shorthand for the divine standard of righteousness we find articulated throughout the Bible, most notably in the Ten Commandments and Christ's Sermon on the Mount. Formally, the Law refers to the various Thou Shalt's and Thou Shalt Not's—commands attached to conditions ("do this and you shall live")—which, taken together, form the shape of divinely mandated holiness.

Martin Luther, taking after the Apostle Paul, understood the Law to be one of the two principal ways God speaks to human beings, the other being the Gospel. If the Law is imperative by nature, the Gospel is indicative ("good *news*"); if the Law commands, the Gospel promises. And yet the Law is not merely a matter of what is said or written; it is a matter of what is *heard*. As such, it cannot be reduced to a moral code or grammatical pattern. This is why Luther characterized the Law as "a voice that man can never stop in this life," one found in equal measure in the deserts of Israel and the manicured lawns of Southern California.[8]

Paul goes so far as to claim that the Law is written on the hearts of all men and women, inborn and part of our DNA, as it were, not terribly

---

8. Luther, quoted in Forde, *Where God Meets Man*, 15.

dissimilar from what Sigmund Freud would later dub the "superego." The entire world exists under its sway. Which may sound overly comprehensive, but even a cursory observation of human nature confirms that, regardless of whether or not a person recognizes the existence God, familiarity with some form of internalized "ought" is unavoidable. In modern parlance, feelings of "not enoughness" inevitably belie some perceived standard of goodness or wholeness at work, some unimpeachable voice of accusation that not even the best-selling American pop group of all time could silence. To paraphrase one of Brian's most vulnerable creations, despite being "blessed with everything," the fears "in the back of my mind" remain.

To be clear, the arbitrary (and often cruel) "oughts" that occupy our inner life are not identical in stature or content to the ones handed down on Mount Sinai. But the two are related and similar in impact. Episcopal theologian Paul Zahl describes it this way:

> In practice, the requirement of perfect submission to the commandments of God is exactly the same as the requirement of perfect submission to the innumerable drives for perfection that drive everyday people's crippled and crippling lives. The commandment of God that we honor our father and mother is no different *in impact*, for example, than the commandment of fashion that a woman be beautiful or the commandment of culture that a man be boldly decisive and at the same time utterly tender.[9]

All this to say, much of the fearful striving that occupies daily life can be traced back to our thorny relationship with the Law, and the judgment it represents. Again, even those who dismiss the existence of the Judge—to say nothing of those of us who outwardly embrace the existence of a God "whose property is always to have mercy"—fear judgment.[10] Irrationally or not, being "frightened of a verdict," as the poet Czesław Miłosz describes in his poem "A Many-Tiered Man," provides a universal touchstone for humanity. We would rather hide than relinquish our defenses; we restlessly maneuver away from what we are confident will be the ensuing condemnation. To the fallen human ear, the tempting response to the Law is redoubled self-assertion, but the only honest one is humility.

Of course, just because Brian couldn't help but allow himself to be seen as weak does not mean he did not struggle with the Law. In fact, the

---

9. Zahl, *Grace in Practice*, 26.
10. Cranmer, "The Prayer of Dr. Cranmer," 136.

dynamic of Law and Gospel can be glimpsed behind both his greatest triumph, *Pet Sounds*, and his most scarring defeat, *SMiLE*.

Pet Sounds catalogs a number of the ways we defend against nakedness, the emotional fig leaves we all sport from time to time. If earlier releases had found Brian trying, unconvincingly, to appease the standards of adolescent cool with glory-rife displays of bravado (e.g. "I Get Around," "Good to My Baby"), *Pet Sounds* adopts a more affecting but no less popular approach, namely, flight. Perhaps it is no coincidence that one of the instrumentals on the record is titled "Let's Go Away For A While," and the final cut, "Caroline No," ends with the sound of a train leaving the station.

Of course, flight can be mental as well as physical. If our reality is deemed unacceptable according to whatever standards of "happiness" we've embraced, we may seek to avoid it through fantasy and wishful thinking, à la "Wouldn't It Be Nice." "If only . . ." is an alluring means of psychological evasion, often masking ongoing resentment, self-directed or otherwise.

An equally potent form of denial can be heard in the victimized self-pity of "I Just Wasn't Made for These Times": "Every time I get the inspiration to go change things around, no one wants to help me look for places where new things might be found." On that remarkable song Brian, via Asher, even attempts to renegotiate the terms of his "acceptance"—"these times" are the problem, not me. Anything but own up to a less-than-ideal here and now!

This is not to suggest that any of this material is one-dimensional, only that, in a certain light, it testifies to an internal agitation in regard to who Brian felt he "ought" to be. The straight male nerd's Judy Garland, indeed.

It may be easier to express gratitude without psychic protection, as "God Only Knows" attests, but rejection hits harder, as would be made painfully clear during the recording and eventual shelving of the follow-up to *Pet Sounds*, the legendary *SMiLE* record. Without the walls we build up to protect ourselves, the voice of the law is quicker to pulverize its hearer. In fact, the entire project would prove to be an object lesson in the fruits of the Law, paralysis and retreat.

The setting in which Brian attempted to record his "teenage symphony to God," as he referred to *SMiLE*, was rife with conflict and pressure. His group had been on the forefront of the American pop landscape for a full four years at that point. Despite the success of "Sloop John B.," *Pet Sounds* did not sell as well as the group was accustomed. Perhaps the subject matter was too far afield from beaches and cars, the atmosphere too melancholy,

You Need a Mess of Help to Stand Alone

the arrangements too baroque for burgeoning hippie sensibilities—who knows. Critics may have hailed it as a masterpiece, but the charts have always been the *lingua franca* of the Beach Boys, and by that measure, the record underperformed. The commercial verdict was fairly condemnatory, which understandably ratchetted up expectations for its successor.

But the pressure was more than commercial. It was artistic, too. Brian has gone on record many times about the competition he felt during those years with the Beatles, whom he viewed not only as an overseas counterpart to the Beach Boys but as the gold standard of pop music, period. Their *Revolver* album was part of the inspiration for the envelope pushing of *Pet Sounds*. Likewise, Paul McCartney famously confessed that *Pet Sounds*, as well as the sonic vanguard it represented, was in the back of his mind while working on *Sgt. Pepper's Lonely Hearts Club Band*. He wanted to beat it.

Brian and Paul and their respective groups were operating in an environment of creative escalation. Of course, unlike the partnership at the core of the Fab Four, Brian was only one person—with an admittedly fragile psychological makeup—whom the press had not been shy about dubbing a "genius." It's no stretch to say that in the face of surpassing *Sgt. Pepper*, that label began to feel less like a compliment and more like a burden. Anything less than a work of genius would be unacceptable.

So despite the stop-gap success of "Good Vibrations," Brian internalized the success of *Sgt. Pepper* as anticipated condemnation, a new standard for him to reach. In other words, the record codified into Law for him: Thou Shalt Be a Genius, and Be One by Outdoing the Beatles. It would turn out to be a bridge too far.

These commercial and artistic pressures were likely compounded by the lack of support Brian received from the band when they returned from touring and heard the initial tapes. Bandmate Mike Love notoriously went on record with his distaste for the avant-garde leanings contained therein. A classic bootlegged recording even finds the singer publicly mocking the words to "Heroes and Villains." Of course, these weren't just bandmates that were rejecting the work; they were family members. One can only assume that the rejection cut deep.

Suffice it to say, these various factors did not foster the atmosphere of creativity and playfulness that the project—indeed, Brian himself—required to persevere.

Those familiar with St. Paul's epistles will not find this sad eventuality surprising. The Law may mandate love (and loving accomplishment), but it has a very hard time inspiring it—at least in the long term. Instead, ironclad expectation tends to stifle self-expression and stimulate second-guessing. As a motivating agent, the law is not just impotent, but counterproductive. In Romans we read that "the law brings wrath," and that the Law was added so that "trespass multiplied" (Rom 4:15, 5:20). Meaning, the Law was not *intended* to deliver what it demands! As St. Augustine once wrote, "The law . . . contributes nothing to God's saving act: through it he does but show man his weakness, that by faith he may take refuge in the divine mercy and be healed."[11]

In any case, when combined with Brian's inner brittleness and the various substances he was abusing at the time, the Law of *SMiLE* triggered a nervous breakdown in its author. In 1967, Brian Wilson retreated to his room for essentially fifteen years. He could not wall himself off emotionally, so he walled himself off physically. Of course, since his talent was so much larger than he was—even at his heaviest (350 pounds!)—it would irrepressibly seep through whatever barriers he tried to erect against it, even during the years he spent "lyin' in bed." His brothers were wise, if a tad optimistic, to build a studio in his house—and ferreting out Brian's passing influence on their largely wonderful early '70s records remains a rewarding hobby.

Still, *SMiLE* would carry painful associations. When asked about the record in subsequent interviews, Brian would avoid the subject and, if pressed, would write it off as "inappropriate music" that nearly killed him. Bad vibrations, in other words, and the beginning of a long period of darkness. One might even conjecture that *SMiLE* came to embody a new kind of Law to Brian, its incompletion casting a shoulda-woulda-coulda shadow over the rest of his career, an indelible testament to failure and weakness, the moment when his vulnerability was met with condemnation and his spirit broken.

Midnight's Another Day: Concluding (Highly) Unscientific Postscript

Nevertheless, a study of the Beach Boys is a study of contradictions, not all of them discouraging. For many pop music fans, *SMiLE* ironically came to serve as shorthand for a different kind of Law: the standard by which all other avant-pop records would be measured, pop music's ultimate "lost masterpiece," its beauty made all the more exquisite by virtue of its

11. Augustine, *Later Works*, 205.

You Need a Mess of Help to Stand Alone

intangibility. After all, there's no better song than the one we've never heard. And the bits that leaked out on Beach Boys albums and boxed sets over the years provided more than enough evidence to justify the hype. "It was like hearing a tape of Mozart," Elvis Costello remarked after hearing a bootleg of the tapes.

Then, the unthinkable happened. In 2004, Brian surprised everyone by resurrecting the project and putting together a completed version of the record, sans Boys. And while perhaps not the earth-shattering opus of imagination, the final product was far from embarrassing. His voice had seen better days, but the self-assurance was palpable, and the release garnered fantastic reviews. On a personal level, it is hard not to view SMiLE 2004 as something of an Easter day, one that came long after, but no less unexpectedly, its Good Friday.

Next, in 2011, the Beach Boys stopped suing each other long enough to put out the tapes of the original sessions. Even in its final incomplete form, SMiLE is a stunning piece of music. Despite the generations of imitators, it still sounds like nothing else: longtime obsessions with Gershwin and Disney were very much germinating; mix in some LSD and "Surfin' Safari," a dash of Mozart, a pinch of Roy Rogers, some Spectorized sea shanty, a hint of Liverpool, even Gregorian chant, and you're almost there. But no description can really do SMiLE justice—this was Brian's vision, not someone else's. The best songs on it ("Cabinessence," "Heroes and Villains," "Surf's Up") outstrip the best songs on Sgt. Pepper's, its most obvious reference point, by a significant margin. What's more, the production is a genuine step forward, tempering the Pet Sounds melancholy with whimsical left turns galore (and thankfully little psychedelic noodling).

Despite a few overly flowery passages, Van Dyke Parks' lyrics are, by and large, distinguished by their wordplay rather than their trippiness. The themes and content are exactly what they had long been rumored to be: the American frontier, the natural world, childhood, physical fitness, humor— one would be hard-pressed to find another record (of the era) with similar thematic breadth. Yet somehow it works, and the *feeling*, which Brian focused on above all else, is indeed a smiling one. Had he been able, in the summer of love, to stare down the Law of the Beatles and put the record out—and he was closer to the finish line than most had assumed—Brian would have indeed set a new bar, and kept the sonic arms race escalating.

And yet, beyond its sheer beauty (and incompleteness), a casual listener could not be faulted for wondering why Brian or anyone would describe the record as a "symphony to God," teenage or otherwise. The Lord gets a mention in "Wonderful" but mainly as a device to deal with adolescent sexuality. Then there's the vaguely Trinitarian Wordsworth quote about the child being the father of the man, which pops up numerous times and dovetails nicely with the inner child theme.

An answer, it turns out, can be found in the album centerpiece "Surf's Up." Those who have heard the original version know that Brian Wilson never sounded more angelic or reverent than he does on that song. In fact, the inspiration is so pronounced that the recording takes on an almost Galilean aspect when you consider the lack of support it garnered at the time.

The liner notes to the re-release of SMiLE reproduce an explanation Brian gave in 1967 of "Surf's Up," shedding new and hopeful light on the song, the project, and even its composer. The words, it turns out, are far more than phonetic window dressing. They point heavenward, beyond the voice of the law and all its ornate finery, to the song beneath every other, that of God's "love and mercy" for his cloudy eyed children:

> "It's a man at a concert," [Brian] said. "All around him there's the audience, playing their roles, dressed up in fancy clothes, looking through opera glasses, but so far away from the drama, from life. Back through the opera glass you see the pit and the pendulum drawn. *The music begins to take over.* Columnated ruins domino. *Empires, ideas, lives, institutions; everything has to fall, tumbling like dominoes. He begins to awaken to the music; sees the pretentiousness of everything.* The music hall a costly bow. Then even the music is gone, *turned into* a trumpeter swan, *into what the music really is.*"
>
> "I heard the word *of God;* Wonderful thing; *the joy of enlightenment, of seeing God. And what is it? A children's song! And then there's the song itself; the song of children; the song of the universe rising and falling in wave after wave, the song of God, hiding the love from us, but always letting us find it again, like a mother singing to her children.*"
>
> *The record was over. Wilson went into the kitchen and squirted Reddi-wip direct from the can into his mouth; made himself a chocolate Great Shake, and ate a couple of candy bars.*[12]

True to form, that final image poses a contradiction that is as amusing as it is poetic. As if to ensure we do not mistake the gift for the Giver, our

---

12. *SMiLE* liner notes.

beloved prodigy, after offering a startlingly articulate (and prophetic) explanation of his art, goes back to swilling junk food. It is enough to make the most jaded listener, well, smile.

Seven

"I See Love"
Perceiving and Building Up Love in *Sunflower*

JEFF SELLARS

The *Sunflower* album appeared amidst success, turmoil, and great change within the Beach Boys. Brian was retreating from work and, subsequently, other band members were stepping forward into the void he left. There were steps forward (successful tours and some chart success) but also many difficult obstacles. The album was released in August of 1970. Just prior to this, there was much activity within the band: they had a minor hit single in 1969, called "Break Away," which was co-written by Brian and his father (under the nom de plum Reggie Dunbar). Brian released

> the album *A World of Peace Must Come*, featuring recitations of poetry by Steve Kalinich . . . over Brian's newly composed (or improvised) back-ground music; [there were] group tours of North America, Europe, and Australia/New Zealand, including a few concerts in early 1970 in which Brian rejoined the group on stage while Mike was hospitalized following a dangerous fast; continued problems for Carl connected with his refusal to join the military draft; continued problems for Dennis resulting in his affiliation with Charles Manson; rumors of financial distress for the group, and Murry's sale of publishing rights for the entire Beach Boys catalogue for $700,000; failed attempts to sign with other record

"I See Love"

labels before settling with Warner Brothers; and the submission of a new Beach Boys album entitled *Add Some Music*, that was rejected by the new label.[1]

Given this instability it is surprising that the minor masterpiece *Sunflower* was created. As Philip Lambert notes, by the time the album was released "a miracle had emerged from the chaos. With solid contributions from Dennis ... and Bruce ... and active participation of all group members in songwriting, performing, and production, the album became a masterpiece of communal spirit and collaborative enterprise."[2] This message of communal spirit, of love, comes through in the music—not least in the very first track of the album. "This Whole World" sets the tone not only of the spirit of the album but also of Brian's way of perceiving, or of his wanting to perceive, his world. The vision is one of love—love as a way of perceiving the world.

At each moment we are perceiving from a particular point of view, putting into focus one thing as others go out of focus. Using painting as an example, Maurice Merleau-Ponty noted this point: "Cezanne ... remarks that 'as soon as you paint you draw,' by which he meant that neither in the world as we perceive it nor in the picture which is an expression of that world can we distinguish absolutely between, on the one hand, the outline or shape of the object and, on the other, the point where colors end or fade ...."[3] This flies in the face of classical approaches to painting—where a painter would create a "conventional representation" of what she sees.[4] So, for example, if painting a landscape, the painter would direct her eyes at, say, a tree in the near distance, then perhaps a road nearby, then finally at the horizon. But each time her eyes move the dimensions change depending on the point of focus. So, the objects in the painting are arranged in a compromise of the varying perspectives—"a common denominator to all these perspectives ...."[5]

But, of course, this is not how we see the world: "at every moment we are forced to adopt a certain point of view ...."[6] As regards music, Tiger Roholt notes that

---

1. Lambert, *Inside the Music*, 302.
2. Ibid.
3. Merleau-Ponty, *World of Perception*, 39.
4. Ibid., 40.
5. Ibid.
6. Ibid.

in order to apprehend one feature of a painting or musical performance, you may need to direct your attention to other features. A rock music critic may write, "The rhythm of this track has an intriguing, frantic quality; in order to hear this, listen to the way the bass guitar repeatedly races ahead of the drums." This may be followed by advice about what not to attend to: "This frantic quality is difficult to hear; if you focus too much on the keyboard and voices, you may fail to hear it." Aesthetic experiences are often active at least in the sense that we can, and often must, look and listen to different features of an artwork.[7]

For Merleau-Ponty, a painting may attempt to present these varying points of view by having different objects "appear" from different perspectives within the same painting: "The lazy viewer will see 'errors of perspective' here, while those who look closely will get the feel of a world in which no two objects are seen simultaneously, a world in which regions of space are separated by the time it takes to move our gaze from one to the other, a world in which being is not given but rather emerges over time."[8] So, space is not to be viewed as a medium of absolute independence or objective perspective but as a medium with a point of view.[9] We are deeply connected to space—but not as pure intellect, as pure disembodied subject. We are beings who dwell in space, relating to it.[10] We are not a mind *and* a body, but a mind *with* a body—beings "who can only get to the truth of things because" our bodies are "embedded in those things."[11]

The band's communal, musical vision of love on this album puts us into a certain focus. Again, as Merleau-Ponty noted in *Sense and Non-Sense*,

> The work of a great novelist always rests on two or three philosophical ideas. For Stendhal, these are the notions of the Ego and Liberty; for Balzac, the mystery of history as the appearance of a meaning in chance events; for Proust, the way the past is involved in the present and the presence of times gone by. The function of

---

7. Roholt, "In Praise of Ambiguity." As an important related aside for this discussion, Tiger Roholt's short paper is an interesting conversation partner—in the way it illustrates a manner of talking about musical experiences that uses Merleau-Ponty's ideas and pushes against a "non-ambiguous" approach to musical receptions.

8. Merleau-Ponty, *World of Perception*, 41.

9. Ibid.

10. Ibid., 42.

11. Ibid., 43.

"I See Love"

the novelist is not to state these ideas thematically but to make them exist for us in the way that things exist.[12]

One major idea that the album *Sunflower* rests upon is love—and the idea of love is made existent for us most explicitly in the lyrics—and in the roles of the voices, instruments, arrangements, and particularities of its presentation, which work at the very least, but not exclusively, in support of these words. This idea of love is not simply or barely stated for us but is shown to us through the musical and lyrical gifts of the band. To cover the entirety of the *Sunflower* album would be too much for our space here. To this end, I will focus on just a few of the songs from *Sunflower*, starting with a more sustained examination of "This Whole World" and then moving on to briefer explorations of "Add Some Music," "All I Wanna Do," "Forever," and "Our Sweet Love." This will be done primarily through Merleau-Ponty's accounts of perception and world building, with occasional help from Gabriel Marcel, and finally landing on the Kierkegaardian notion of love as up-building.

This Whole World

The opening line of "This Whole World" leaves no doubt for the listener about Brian's concerns and the scope of those concerns—he is thinking about this whole world, and what does he see when he looks at the world? He sees love. When speaking of the song, Brian notes,

> It's one of my very favorites. Structurally, it rambles, but I just remember I said (at the time it was first recorded), "Listen, this is a really spiritual tune." We double-tracked our singing on that one; but we always double-tracked our voices, always. Carl sang the lead and I did the voices in the background. It was inspired by my love of the world, how I love people, and how people should be free.[13]

The pulsating guitar intro accentuates the biting beginning vocal phrase. The drums fall in with a fill and the song is off to an energetic start. The drums lean into the rhythm of the track, pushing it into a bouncy groove: the active, hippity bass drum and the tom-toms keep the song tripping forward. The song does not simply "settle in" to its groove—and the constant

---

12. Merleau-Ponty, *Sense and Non-Sense*, 26.
13. White, *Sunflower/Surf's Up*.

modulation of the melody is a clue to the restless nature of the song's lyrics. We are told repeatedly, for example, what the singer sees (in the refrain at the end of the main melody line, a total of three times)—he sees love. It needs repeating as a focus of importance and as a reminder to the listener—but also as a convincing element to the singer and not merely as some bare statement of fact.

We are taken from specific instances and sentiments (girls getting mad at boys for a "show," where the true nature of love lies beneath these facades) to general sentiments (we are "everywhere" like "everyone"). This finally leads to the presentation of action—it's another day to display "your love," to take these ways of perceiving the world and apply them in your life. Brian is working an argument that references the specific instances of love—the "mundane" aspects of puppy love—and connecting them to the more abstract sense of connection that we have with the whole world. We cannot separate ourselves from this world. This "abstract" notion is then brought back down into the specific, the world we live in, by imploring us to act on this realization, to bring this love into "another day." The vocal breakdown at the end of the song drops us back into contemplation—where we think about the love in this whole world—punctuated by the meditative and stirring "Ahoom bop didits" as they fade out. The song communicates its perspective through the use of simple lyrical turns, complex chord modulations, exciting drumming, and intricate harmony. This communication asks us to change our perspective, too. As Marcel noted,

> At the moment when communication is established between me and the other, however, we pass from one world into another; we emerge into a region where one is not merely one among others, where transcendence takes on the aspect of love. The category of the given is transcended; "never enough, always more, always closer"; these are the simple expressions which clearly indicate the change of perspective I am trying to evoke . . . .[14]

The other, then, as an other, transcends this otherness, to "take on the aspect of love," and becomes more than just "one among many": the other is now a *thou*—and we, too, in turn become a thou through this process. The given is transcended in the moreness of this perspective—we can always move deeper into the other.

There is an intimate connection between the life of the mind and the life of the body here that betrays dualistic notions. To come back to

---

14. Marcel, *Creative Fidelity*, 72.

"I See Love"

Merleau-Ponty, and set the Beach Boys aside for a moment, things are not neutral objects that we contemplate; they present (symbolize or recall) ways of behaving—that we react to, favorably or unfavorably.[15] People's reactions then become decipherable to us by the objects with which they surround themselves.[16] The objects in dreams, for example, are also informative for the same reason: objects speak to our bodies and lives. The essence of things, then, can be found in what they can say to us.[17] This relationship is not clear cut, however: "vertiginous proximity prevents us both from apprehending ourselves as a pure intellect separate from things and from defining things as pure objects lacking all human attributes."[18]

This also allows us to expand our interests and recognize the importance of other perspectives (e.g., that of animals). Rather than seeing these other perspectives as *automata* or deficient (from so-called normal human perspective) we should instead set the questions to these perspectives within their own particular settings: the world of the dog is to be seen through its own positioning—if we set the dog tasks from our own positioning (e.g., unlocking a door, reading a book) we might merely see the dog as absurd or mechanical.[19]

Descartian dualistic notions of pure spirit as altogether different from pure matter can tend to separate us from our bodies, but in contrast Merleau-Ponty argued, "It is clear that I can only find and, so to speak, touch this absolutely pure spirit in myself."[20] We only know other beings through their bodies—other humans are "never pure spirit for me."[21] We only know others

> through their glances, their gestures, their speech.... Of course *another human being* is certainly more than simply a body to me.... Yet I cannot detach someone from their silhouette, the tone of their voice and its accent.... Another person, for us, is a spirit which haunts a body and we seem to see a whole host of possibilities contained within this body when it appears before us; the body is the very presence of these possibilities. So the process of looking

---

15. Merleau-Ponty, *World of Perception*, 48.
16. Ibid.
17. Ibid., 49.
18. Ibid., 51.
19. Ibid., 58.
20. Ibid., 62.
21. Ibid.

at human beings from the outside—that is, at other people—leads us to reassess a number of distinctions which once seemed to hold good such as that between mind and body.²²

Merleau-Ponty uses anger as an example for this. If one is angry with an interlocutor, that anger is expressed through that person's body—the dilated eyes, the tone of voice, the purple cheeks, the movement of hands, the contortions of the face, etc. The anger is in the body. People will say that the anger is in the mind of that person, but this is simply apparent. The anger is discerned through those bodily gestures and gesticulations—not in some "otherworldly realm":

> It is in the space between him and me that it unfolds. I would accept that the sense in which the place of my opponent's anger is on his face is not the same as that in which, in a moment, tears may come streaming from his eyes or a grimace may harden on his mouth. Yet anger inhabits him and it blossoms on the surface of his pale or purple cheeks, his blood-shot eyes and wheezing voice . . . .²³

This is also so if we look inward at our own reactions. What is it like for you when you are angry? We cannot find an element to be separated from our bodies; when we are angry it is not that the anger lies somewhere outside the body (as if only in our minds, among our thoughts); rather, it is there, between you and the one at whom your anger is directed. Only after the anger subsides do we then take time to "reflect on what anger is and remark that it involves a certain (negative) evaluation of another person" and conclude that anger is "a thought; to be angry is to think that the other person is odious and his thought, like all others, cannot—as Descartes has shown—reside in any piece of matter and therefore must belong to the mind."²⁴ One might be content to think thusly until one turns again to the actual experience and realizes that the connection between the anger and the body cannot be severed; thought and body are inexplicably bound up together.

We are as children bound up not in our self-consciousness but in the experience of other people.²⁵ We become aware of our existence through

---

22. Ibid., 62–63.
23. Ibid., 63.
24. Ibid., 64.
25. Ibid., 65.

"I See Love"

contact with others, and this contact is "always mediated by a particular culture, or at least by a language that we have received from without and which guides our self-knowledge."[26] The ideal of a pure intellect is useful as a critical lens through which to view the unfiltered influx of the world, but "such a self only develops into a free agent by way of the instrument of language and by taking part in the life of the world."[27] We are not then an "aggregate" of individual thinking things, "guaranteed from the outset to be able to reach agreement with the others because all participate in the same thinking essence"—nor are we a single "Being in which the multiplicity of individuals are dissolved and into which these individuals are destined to be reabsorbed."[28] Humanity's position is precarious:

> each person can only believe [she or he] recognizes to be true internally and, at the same time, nobody thinks or makes up [his or her] mind without already being caught up in certain relationships with others,[29] which leads [her or him] to opt for a particular set of opinions. Everyone is alone and yet nobody can do without other people, not just because they are useful . . . but also when it comes to happiness. There is no way of living with others which takes away the burden of being myself, which allows me to not have an opinion; there is no "inner" life that is not a first attempt to relate to another person. In this ambiguous position, which has been forced on us because we have a body and a history (both personally and collectively), we can never know complete rest. We are continually obliged to work on our differences, to explain things we have said that have not been properly understood, to reveal what is hidden within us and to perceive other people. Reason does not lie behind us, nor is that where the meeting of minds takes place: rather, both stand before us waiting to be inherited.

26. Ibid., 66.
27. Ibid.
28. Ibid.
29. Gabriel Marcel's notions of self-knowledge and knowledge of others can be related to Merleau-Ponty's ideas of being caught up in relationships with others, of being connected in an intimate way. For Marcel, this presents itself as a paradox: "The paradox is that at the same time it is also my own personal experience that I rediscover in some way, for in reality my experience is in a real communication with other experiences . . . . It is because the egoist confines his thought to himself that he is fundamentally in the dark about himself . . . . A complete and concrete knowledge of oneself cannot be heautocentric . . . . The fact is that we can understand ourselves by starting from the other, or from others, and only by starting from them . . ." (Marcel, *Mystery of Being*, 7–8).

Yet we are no more able to reach them definitively than we are to give up on them.[30]

Merleau-Ponty makes reference to painting throughout *The World of Perception* because for him painting brings us into contact with objects we think we know well (lemons, landscapes, trees, etc.) but in a way that defies our "normal" apprehension of them. Art holds our gaze in a way that makes us ask questions, makes us look to the very essence of things. Art brings us back again to the world, but in a renewed fashion.

The idea that we can separate things from their way of appearing is not possible. We may think that when we have defined an object, such as a table, by its denotative properties, we have somehow gotten to its essence ("a horizontal flat surface supported by three or four legs"), but when we have done this move we have removed ourselves from all of the "accidental properties" that share in its essence (its particular color, the "shape of the feet, the style of the moulding and so on").[31] When we remove ourselves in this way we are not perceiving but defining—for when we perceive the table we do not separate ourselves from the particular elements of the table. It is the details that give us pause and give rise to the abstraction "table": "No detail is insignificant: the grain, the shape of the feet, the color and age of the wood, as well as the scratches or graffiti which show that age. The meaning, 'table,' will only interest me insofar as it arises out of all the 'details' which embody its present mode of being."[32]

Art, too, is bound by this particularity, by its details. Art is revealed to us through those details. If art is merely a signifier, a purely representational move, then its meaning would rest outside the work of art—in the things it signifies ("in its subject").[33] With music, Merleau-Ponty noted that, in this case, it is

> impossible . . . to make out that the work of art refers to anything other than itself; programmatic music, which describes a storm or even an occasion of sadness, is the exception. Here we are unquestionably in the presence of an art form that does not speak. And yet a piece of music comes very close to being no more than a medley of sound sensations: from among these sounds we discern the appearance of a phrase and, as phrase follows phrase, a whole

---

30. Merleau-Ponty, *World of Perception*, 66–67.
31. Ibid., 70.
32. Ibid.
33. Ibid., 71.

"I See Love"

and, finally, as Proust put it, a world. This world exists in the universe of possible music, whether in the district of Debussy or the kingdom of Bach.[34]

Merleau-Ponty is here suggesting that the special content-form relation is explicit in music—in that it demonstrates the "process of expression" bringing "meaning into being" and thus "does not merely translate it."[35] Of course, popular music adds lyrics into this mixture, and Merleau-Ponty points to Mallarme to get at the distinctiveness of poetic language. In everyday language, in everyday "chatter," one names things in order to get at them quickly and convey them quickly, to let people know what one is talking about; poetic language, however, does not—it precisely brings one out of the ordinary, "well-knownness," of things into a relationship with the essence of the things presented. So, poetry brings us not to the world of ideas or signifiers but to the world presented—into a place where form and content cannot be separated. Again, Merleau-Ponty highlighted this deep connection between form and content in *Phenomenology of Perception*, with music as a primary example: "The musical meaning of a sonata is inseparable from the sounds which are its vehicle: before we have heard it no analysis enables us to anticipate it; once the performance is over, we shall, in our intellectual analyses of the music, be unable to do anything but carry ourselves back to the moment of experiencing it."[36]

With the Beach Boys' music, and with "This Whole World" in particular, we are analyzing something that must be experienced; we must come back to the music, back to the world that the musician has created. Brian is thinking about this whole world—but which world? The world of love that he sees and that he wants us to see and wants us to create with him.

Add Some Music

As the a cappella coda of "This Whole World" ends, the jangling guitar of "Add Some Music" soon fades in, and the obvious connection here is made for us at the outset: the song explicitly connects the soul to the "Sunday mornin' Gospel," historically, practically, and emotionally. The simple plea of adding music to our day, and its potential for making us "come together

---

34. Ibid., 74–75.
35. Merleau-Ponty, *Phenomenology of Perception*, 213.
36. Ibid., 212.

as one," betrays the deep, soulful connection the middle change-up evokes. The mundane occurrences of our musical daily lives—music at the dentist's office, in weddings, on phones, in movies, coming from ice cream trucks—are certainly portrayed as ways in which music permeates those daily activities. But when Carl intones that music is in his soul, there is no doubt that this plea is not a call for a merely mundane apprehension of music in everyday life; rather, it is a call to let music—even the "background music"—penetrate the soul of the listener. This deep connection is the way to a loving perception of the world—of potentially making us one. It has to be felt from within this framework if it is to carry that effect into the world. It is not a naïve conception that music played anywhere will cause peace, love, and understanding. It is a plea to see music as the deep, soul-satisfying medium that Brian sees and feels it to be.

All I Wanna Do

The bed of sound upon which "All I Wanna Do" rests is an unsettled oceanic washing and swaying: the laid-back, heavy drums, smothered in echo; the buried lead vocal, just barely rising above the background, almost drowning in the wash; the slap-back delay on the backing vocals. The whole song is laying back into the uncertainty of the singer's control. Mike Love's voice is calm and apparently presenting a settling element in contrast to the oceanic feel of the music—he is promising continued support and love in spite of the uncertainty of the world: his love is as sure as the sun rising (seemingly unaware of any Humean doubts about this supposed certainty) and it burns brightly like the moon and stars.

The idea of love as certain is complicated, no doubt, and, accordingly, the song presents this by way of mood and delivery if not by way of direct lyric. Paradoxically, this uncertainty is estimated as certainty from the lover, with more uncertainties and reservations and all that this entails: as Merleau-Ponty would have it, "It is therefore of the essence of certainty to be established only with reservations."[37] And, so, Mike reiterates that this is all he wants to do—to give love—but the rhythm and feel of the song adds uncertainty to the promise, undermining his promise. The backing vocals echo the promises of the singer, but they too are in the general wash of the song, swathed in slap-back echo, emanating from deep down in the mix, shouting within that general wash while at the same time pushing

37. Ibid., 461.

"I See Love"

against it—both thematically (through its push of certainty) and practically (by way of the odd slap-back echo timing and its thickening of the vocal sound).

The world created here begs us to see the certainty of love within this set of reservations, and to assert that certainty nonetheless. The mood of the music, and the play of the lyrics in conjunction with it, allows the listener to feel along with the singer.

Forever

Brian's description of Dennis's beautifully simple song is telling: "'Forever' has to be the most harmonically beautiful thing I've ever heard,' Brian now declares. 'It's a rock and roll prayer.'"[38]

Dennis's calm, slightly raspy delivery adds a sense of tiredness, worry, and importance to the performance. The calm seems to come directly from this tiredness and worry—as if he'd been up all night crying, contemplating how he might pass his heartfelt feeling along. The tone, rasp, and volume of his voice also add to this effect—it pulls one's attention to it by its smallness. Dennis tells his lover that the various gifts he has would be given forever if he could but muster the strength and endurance. This reflects the completeness of the gift of love and works in conjunction with the deep stillness of his voice.

Dennis is here making the declaration that he in some sense belongs to his beloved—a commitment is made, rather than the stark claim of possession, "you belong to me." The distinction is an important one. As Marcel pointed out,

> The most important characteristic of these statements would be lost if we consider either one as an assertion although at the limit they are reducible to this . . . . To take a specific example, we may envisage what takes place between two lovers. A woman says to a man: you belong to me. It is clear that this affirmation may be classified as either a claim or an assertion . . . . The man who is the object of the claim is degraded by it to the rank of a slave . . . unless it is inwardly compensated for somehow by a "but I on the other hand belong to you," i.e., by a commitment. Taken by itself, the claim is despotic. I can do what I want with you, whatever I please. If it is inwardly compensated for, its meaning, its virulence,

---

38. White, *Sunflower/Surf's Up*.

> are attenuated. Since I belong to you as you belong to me, I cannot wish to make you anything other than what you wish for yourself . . . . From that moment on, I cannot even decide whether it would not be better for you not to belong to me. To be more accurate, since I cease to belong to myself, it is not literally true to say that you belong to me; we transcend one another in the very heart of *our love*.[39]

The last stanza reflects the finitude of his embodied promises and his finite situation—he is going away. He cannot maintain the strength, endurance—indeed, the life force needed to fulfill these promises. But he also tantalizingly hints at something more, beyond his finitude—he's not gone forever. Of course, this is a reference to the coming and going of regular life, the leaving and returning of a lover from his work. But the heavenly hymnlike nature of the song, and the rising vocal cues, give a sense of something haunting the background of the song and this notion in particular. There is continuation; the love lasts forever. The world built in this song asks us to stretch our concept of love beyond a merely physical notion of *eros* to a promise of *agape*.

Our Sweet Love

Lastly, we come to "Our Sweet Love." This is the antepenultimate song on the album, and, as with so many Brian Wilson compositions,[40] this is a deceptively simple love song. But much is going on under the surface of this simple love song. For example, the complicated chord structure can pass unnoticed for some—so adept at making these difficult changes is Brian that they can appear easy:

> the bass lines of both verse and chorus of "Our Sweet Love" move mostly by half step . . . [in] *chromatic* descents . . . . Further, the bass descents in "Our Sweet Love" are also used to generate key changes, between verse in G major and chorus in E major (down a minor third, as in many *Pet Sounds* key changes). And as always, the shifts are executed with seemingly effortless grace.[41]

---

39. Marcel, *Creative Fidelity*, 97–99.

40. This song was co-written with Carl Wilson and Al Jardine, but it still displays very identifiable and characteristic Brian Wilson songwriting traits, as seen in the following Philip Lambert quote.

41. Lambert, *Inside the Music*, 304.

"I See Love"

Again, we see the trademark melodic modulations, the complex chord changes and harmonies underlying the deceptively simple words and the beautiful melody. The words, as in "Forever," hint at making something finite—a love affair—into something beyond the finite: their love could last forever. The singer reflects upon the world, observing the things present to him—a summer day, incense and flowers, a winter night—seeing that these things have been made in love and yet are finite. Still, this love "should" last forever. A touch of lament lingers in the lyrics and in bits of the melody—the quick modifying chord changes create a sense of uncertainty here as well: the melodic ground is shifting under our feet. But the pervasive message still breaks through—love should last forever, and there is hope.

The feeling of love expressed here is expressed as a reality that cannot be denied by the lover. The lover is overcome with the reality of that love. This has dangers, of course. Merleau-Ponty noted that, for example,

> love and will are inner operations; they forge their own objects, and it is clear that in doing so they may be sidetracked from reality and, in that sense, mislead us; but it seems impossible that they should mislead us about themselves. From the moment I feel love, joy or sadness, it is the case that I love, that I am joyful or sad, even when the object does not in fact (that is, for others or for myself at other times) have the value that I now attribute to it. Appearance is, within me, reality, and the being of consciousness consists in appearing to itself.[42]

There is a sense in which the immediacy of perception places the reality directly before our eyes: the moment we feel love it is the case that we love. When we are in the listening experience we can also participate in these feelings conveyed through the music and lyrics. When the Beach Boys express their love or recount a love story, we too can feel along with them, alter our perceptions, be in line with another mode of thinking and being. This is not to say, however, that we cannot have "true" feelings and "false" feelings, or simply believe that we are in love when we are in fact not. Merleau-Ponty continues:

> There can never be illusion other than with regard to the external object. A feeling, considered in itself, is always true once it is felt .... It is, in the first place, quite clear that we are able to discriminate, within ourselves, between "true" and "false" feelings, that everything felt by us as within ourselves is not *ipso facto* placed on a

---

42. Merleau-Ponty, *Phenomenology of Perception*, 439.

single footing of existence, or true in the same way, and that there are degrees of reality within us as there are, outside of us, "reflections," "phantoms" and "things." Besides true love, there is false or illusory love. This last case must be distinguished from misinterpretations, and those errors in which I have deceitfully given the name of love to emotions unworthy of it. For in such cases there was never even a semblance of love, and never for a moment did I believe that my life was committed to that feeling. I conspired with myself to avoid asking the question in order to avoid receiving the reply which was already known to me; my "love"-making was an attempt to do what was expected of me, or merely deception. In mistaken or illusory love, on the other hand, I was willingly united to the loved one, she was for a time truly the vehicle of my relationships with the world. When I told her that I loved her, I was not "interpreting," for my life was in truth committed to a form which, like a melody, demanded to be carried on.[43]

In this sense, "Our Sweet Love" is presenting and advocating for its perception of love, as does the entire album. It is, as it were, an exercise in up-building for its audience—i.e., in building up that perception of love for the listener. We assume, perhaps sometimes wrongly—and especially with pop artists—that works of art are presented to us not simply for the mere selfish presentation of the artist, but also for the possible connection it can make to its audience. In this case, Brian and the Beach Boys do present their music as not just a mere solipsistic exhibition but a possible agent for change and connection. When speaking of his songs in general, Brian often talks about them in spiritual terms. As just one example, when speaking of "Cool, Cool Water" on this album, he notes, "'Well, I'm proud of 'Cool, Cool Water' . . . because that was a divinely inspired song. I had just moved into a new house on Bellagio Road in Bel Air, in March of 1967, and the first day I moved in, there was a piano there, and I went to the piano and wrote 'Cool, Cool Water.'"[44] The message the Beach Boys chiefly convey in this album is one of love—and when coupled with Brian's vision of pop music and his mission "to spread the gospel of love through records," we see the desire for up-building.[45]

For Kierkegaard, too, the purpose of building up is love. As Kierkegaard noted, "*building up* is exclusively characteristic of love . . . . The

43. Ibid., 439–40.
44. White, *Sunflower/Surf's Up*.
45. Wilson, "Music is God's Voice."

"I See Love"

characteristic is just this that it exclusively has the attribute of complete self-giving. There is nothing, nothing, which cannot be done or said in such a way that it becomes up-building, but whatever it is, if it does build up, then love is present."[46] Love is present in this song, in this album. The up-building is present in Brian's push to perceive "this whole world" in love; it is present in the soulful cry of Carl Wilson that music is in his soul and he wants it to be in yours as well, to see the connectedness of all humankind; it is present in Mike's mournful plea to his lover that all he wants to do is "always bring love to you"; it is present in Dennis's promise of forever; and it is present here, even in the seeming mundanity of our sweet love. The band is building up a view of love, from the ground up, and, as Kierkegaard noted,

> To build up is to construct something from the ground up. In the simple illustration of a house, a building, everyone knows what is meant by ground and foundation. But spiritually understood, what are the ground and foundation of the life of the spirit which are to bear the building? In very fact it is love; love is the origin of everything, and spiritually understood love is the deepest ground of the life of the spirit. Spiritually understood, the foundation is laid in every person in whom there is love. And the edifice which, spiritually understood, is to be constructed, is again love; and it is love which edifies. Love builds up, and it is this which love builds up.[47]

---

46. Kierkegaard, *Works of Love*, HarperCollins, 202.
47. Ibid., 204–5.

Eight

Apocalypse of Love
The Event of *Pet Sounds* in Process Perspective

AUSTIN J. ROBERTS

Introduction

The image—and it is but an image—the image under which . . . God's nature is best conceived, is that of a tender care that nothing be lost . . . . He is the poet of the world, with tender patience leading it by his vision of truth, beauty, and goodness.

(Alfred North Whitehead)[1]

Love is here today and it's gone tomorrow.

(The Beach Boys)[2]

During the 1960s, one of the greatest American rock bands and most influential American theologians of the twentieth century both began to blossom in their careers. The musical characters of this story are the Beach Boys, who worked in various Los Angeles recording studios to

---

1. Whitehead, *Process and Reality*, 346.
2. The Beach Boys, *Pet Sounds*.

Apocalypse of Love

eventually release *Pet Sounds* in 1966. Today, most of their fans and critics continue to claim that it is their most important album. Particularly in its use of unconventional instruments and found sounds, such as bicycle bells, clashing soda cans, barking dogs, and trains, *Pet Sounds* was a truly revolutionary album in the history of music. Along with its complex layers of sound and rich vocal harmonies, the album's lyrical themes often express anxiety about the loss of youth and a desire for love to somehow be grounded in a deeper wisdom. With its brilliant creativity and perennially relevant lyrics, one should not underestimate the massive influence that *Pet Sounds* has had on rock and pop music since it was released. *Rolling Stone* magazine has named it the second greatest album of all time (just behind the Beatles' *Sgt. Pepper's Lonely Hearts Club Band*, which was itself partly inspired by *Pet Sounds*) and claimed that it suggested "a new grown-up identity for rock & roll music itself" with its "vivid orchestration, lyrical ambition, elegant pacing and thematic coherence...."[3]

Not far from the recording studios where *Pet Sounds* was recorded is the small town of Claremont, which is where we encounter the theological character of this story, John B. Cobb Jr. As one of the leading process theologians in the country at Claremont School of Theology, Cobb significantly influenced twentieth-century theology after he published *A Christian Natural Theology* in 1965. Although process theology is often thought to be overwhelmingly complicated, Cobb's Christian process theology can be most simply understood as an attempt to take the biblical notion that God is love (1 John 4:8) as seriously as possible. He thus proposed a radically *relational* image of creation in which God and the world mutually influence one another, divine power is essentially persuasive rather than coercive, and the future is open—even for God. Although some of these ideas appeared in older theologies, Cobb's important development of process theism has left few corners of liberal and progressive theology untouched. The historical theologian Gary Dorrien has even claimed that process theology is "the one indispensable school of thought for progressive theology as a whole."[4] As the foremost pioneer of process theology, Cobb is thus undoubtedly a major figure for Christian theology over the last fifty years. In fact, Dorrien calls him the most admirable North American theologian, not only because of his influential work in philosophical theology, but also because of his

---

3. "500 Greatest Albums of All Time."
4. Dorrien, "David Griffin's Whiteheadian Religious Philosophy," 17.

tireless efforts "to advance the cause of social justice and the flourishing of life."[5]

So what do the Beach Boys and John Cobb have in common, other than a shared interest in the theme of love and their peculiarly intersecting histories? If I might be so bold, I want to suggest that both the release of *Pet Sounds* and Cobb's groundbreaking development of process theology each unleashed an *event*. The notion of an event has gained traction in recent times, particularly amongst postmodern philosophers and theologians. The singularity and surprise of such events rupture and transform our "horizon of expectations"—in these cases, about Western music and Christian theology.[6] To use more explicitly theological language, perhaps we might also call an event an *apocalypse*. To be sure, this sense of an apocalypse does not suggest the end of the world, but rather, following the original Greek meaning, an unveiling or disclosure of something that was previously hidden. Rather than bringing *closure* to history, an apocalypse suggests *dis*closure: a new and unanticipated *opening* for life to prosper.[7]

As such, it seems to me that the similarly apocalyptic character of both *Pet Sounds* and Cobb's work offers an interesting opportunity to theologically evaluate a number of connections between them. In this essay, I will therefore explore the implications of this unusual entanglement between a rock band and a Christian theologian, suggesting some ways that Cobb's process theology might interpret the musical experiments and existential lyrics that the Beach Boys produced with *Pet Sounds*. Perhaps this experiment will theologically illuminate certain aspects of *Pet Sounds*, and even open up new ways of listening to the album as a whole. I am not interested in merely digging up spiritual themes in unexpected places, but in something more radical. By reframing our experience of music within an alternative *cosmology*—a musicosmology, perhaps, that places feeling, creativity, and Beauty at the center of its vision—might we begin to encounter music in more profound ways? In order to illustrate this possibility, the first part of this essay will involve a philosophical journey into the heart of Cobb's aesthetically driven theo-cosmology. Developing out of his process perspective is the provocative metaphor of God as "*creative-responsive love*," which will provide the basis for the rest of my discussion.

---

5. Dorrien, "The Lure and Necessity of Process Theology," 333.
6. Caputo, *The Insistence of God*, 10.
7. Keller, *Apocalypse Now and Then*, ix, 1.

Apocalypse of Love

Exploring the "creative" side of God's love in part two, I will then argue that Cobb's theology points beyond the specious sacred-secular divide that is sometimes erected by Christians, particularly in relation to the arts. This will involve an explanation of his notion of *creative transformation*: a process in which God, as "poet of the world," introduces novel possibilities into creation to lure contradictions into complex contrasts. Creative transformation can be occasionally glimpsed in certain bursts of complex aesthetic intensity in history, which Cobb interprets as God's future arriving in the present as a gift—or even, we might say, as apocalyptic disclosures of Godself out of pure love for her creation. And for Cobb, it is the cosmic Christ who is the agent of creative transformation, so Christians speak of a kenotic love in particular: a risky offer of Godself to every moment that can always be rejected. As such, one might imagine *Pet Sounds* as an instance of Christ's creative immanence within the arts, and even as a micro-apocalypse of love that generated new artistic possibilities. Perhaps we can then begin to see the significance of Christ in new ways.

In part three, I will conclude by exploring the "responsive" love of God in relation to certain existential lyrical themes in *Pet Sounds* that resonate with Cobb's process perspective. Just as *Pet Sounds* tends to express a struggle over the loss of youth and the immediacy of love, Cobb understands the "problem of perpetual perishing" to pose a deep challenge for human existence. The very fact that everything ultimately fades into the past creates a profound crisis of meaning, according to Cobb, for nothing seems to ground our values or individual and collective achievements in history. Because he views this nihilistic threat as a more basic problem to overcome than even physical death, Cobb developed a theology of God's responsive love to provide an eschatological release from this predicament. For him, only a God who genuinely *experiences* the world's joys and sufferings can offer salvation from our condition of perpetual perishing. As such, the responsive love of God becomes the ground of new creation and resurrection for Cobb, as we will ultimately see.

Part I: Cobb's Theo-cosmology

Process philosophy originated in the thinking of the British mathematician and philosopher Alfred North Whitehead in the early twentieth century. It would only later become the inspiration for Christian process theology in the mid-twentieth century. After studying with another great process philosopher, Charles Hartshorne, Cobb went on to become one of the leaders of American process theology and to teach many of the leading process theologians of later generations. His argument that Christian theologians should return to a form of natural theology via Whitehead's metaphysics was a controversial position at a time when neo-orthodoxy had cast deep suspicions upon philosophical theology as a whole. His realist commitment to relational theism also went against the death of God theologies that were becoming more influential in the academy.[8] Against these alternatives, Cobb insisted that natural theology remains necessary, in part because he believed that even theologians who explicitly claim to reject it are inevitably presupposing metaphysical positions.[9] As such, Whitehead's philosophy gave Cobb a way to affirm the particularity of Christian faith without rejecting other sources of knowledge, and also to think of divine action in a meaningful way that maintains a robust sense of creaturely freedom.

The basic claim of Cobb's process metaphysics is that everything is composed of internally related and momentary events, or "actual occasions of experience." His dynamic, lively, and relational ontology thus opposes a materialist claim that the basic real things in nature are lifeless bits of impenetrable matter, and displaces the static philosophical category of substance.[10] Furthermore, every actual occasion has some element of *experience*—not necessarily *conscious* experience, but some modicum of freedom to respond to its environmental influences in one way or another.[11] This nonconscious experience, or "feeling," by which an occasion internalizes its influences to become something new is what Whitehead called "prehension."[12]

By prehending both its immediate and distant past, each occasion develops as a unique aesthetic synthesis of its internalized influences. In a fully interconnected cosmology, this includes the entire past of the universe in varying degrees of intensity. As Cobb explains:

> Each actual occasion comes into being against the background of the whole past of the world. That past is composed of innumerable actual occasions that had their moment of subjective "immediacy" and have "perished." As perished, they have not become

8. Dorrien, "Dialectics of Difference," 234.
9. Cobb, *A Christian Natural Theology*, xv.
10. Ibid., 11.
11. Cobb and Griffin, *Process Theology*, 17.
12. Ibid., 19.

simply nothing. Rather they have their own mode of being, which Whitehead calls "objective immortality." That means that they are effective as objects to be prehended by new occasions. They are the efficient causes explaining why the new occasions embody the characteristics that they do in fact have.[13]

This does not mean that occasions are fully determined by their past. Every occasion is capable of some degree of freedom, to be its own final cause, which allows it to synthesize its influences in a unique way. An occasion begins by receiving its influences and then makes a particular aesthetic decision about how to synthesize them for its own concrete becoming.[14] The final synthesis of past influences is what is called the present occasion's "satisfaction." After its satisfaction, the occasion "perishes" and becomes a new potential for future occasions.

This ubiquitous relational process of becoming in which "the many become one and are increased by one" is what constitutes *everything* in creation: from rocks, trees, and mountains to birds, humans, and musical instruments.[15] For Cobb, whatever endures through time in any way is a uniquely related series or stream of occasions, although the everyday things that we experience with our senses are distinctly interrelated webs or "societies" of occasions.[16] As such, even though many things seem to have a kind of static permanence to our ordinary senses, Cobb believes that this is an *abstraction* that we tend to mistake for concrete reality. Everything is therefore composed of complex and interconnected processes of becoming rather than individual substances that remain essentially static through time.

Cobb's ontology thus entails a rejection of both monism and dualism, which has important implications for how we understand the human creature. While the mind and body are distinct, they are not two substances (as Descartes believed), but neither are they reduced to one thing (as in reductionist materialisms). For Cobb, the mind or soul is a series of occasions like everything else. It is distinct only in terms of its complexity and intensity as the organizing center of living animals and is related to the body in a mutually influential fashion.[17] Cobb also believes that the physical and mental

13. Cobb, *A Christian Natural Theology*, 11–12.
14. Cobb and Griffin, *Process Theology*, 20.
15. Whitehead, *Process and Reality*, 21.
16. Cobb, *A Christian Natural Theology*, 13.
17. Cobb and Griffin, *Process Theology*, 88.

are two "poles" of every occasion, varying in their function depending on the type of entity in question. That is, all occasions are dipolar: the "physical pole" prehends *past actualities* while the "mental pole" prehends *future possibilities*, which provide a suggestive pattern for how an occasion might synthesize its influences in a novel way. By prehending these future possibilities, which Whitehead names "eternal objects," an occasion is thereby capable of becoming something new in history rather than merely repeating past achievements.[18] With Whitehead, Cobb is convinced that because we can think of things not actualized in the world, there must be such a world of ideal potentialities alongside the world of actualities: "ideas need not have concrete reference," Cobb writes.[19]

But how are the eternal objects incorporated into the world? How does the new become actual if it does not simply grow out of the past? In the first place, Cobb explains this occurrence through the freedom inherent in all actual occasions. For some occasions, the physical pole is primary (e.g., those constituting rocks), which makes their freedom trivial. Because their mental pole is virtually irrelevant, they basically repeat their past with little variation. On the other hand, some occasions (e.g., those constituting human minds) with increased mentality have more freedom, and are thus able to include and harmonize more of their past by actualizing eternal objects of greater complexity.[20] Without the prehension of such novel possibilities, we humans would be creatures entirely of our past, and thus neither living nor genuinely free. In the initial phase of an occasion's becoming, it receives influences from its past and is lured toward ideal possibilities for its completion. Whether it aligns with an ideal possibility or not, every occasion makes a subjective choice about how to aesthetically synthesize its influences to become itself.[21] The final result of its decision for or against certain ideals can range from dull repetition to astonishing novelty.

The second way in which possibilities become actual is where we encounter Cobb's relational theism. If the non-actual eternal objects are necessarily *given* in a *limited* way to occasions in every new moment, logically there must be a unique actuality in the cosmic process to accomplish this. This requires further explanation. First, Cobb argues that only the actual, and not the possible, is agential. Eternal objects have no power in

18. Cobb, *A Christian Natural Theology*, 6, 8.
19. Ibid., 98.
20. Cobb and Griffin, *Process Theology*, 73.
21. Cobb, *A Christian Natural Theology*, 9.

Apocalypse of Love

themselves to *do* anything, even though their existence must somehow be accounted for. Cobb therefore asserts that they constitute the "mind" (or mental pole) of a unique actuality.[22] Second, eternal objects must also be ordered in some sense, for despite a great deal of spontaneity in nature, the infinite possibilities for the world's becomings cannot be actualized at random. Because creation undeniably appears as a relatively ordered, limited phenomenon (i.e., it could have been otherwise) and not as a chaotic, "indiscriminate . . . pluralism," eternal objects require not just agency, but *limitation*.[23] As such, Cobb argues that God is that unique actuality which provides the world with its fluid sense of order and novelty. By ordering the eternal objects within the divine life according to their values for each momentary occasion, God's provision of novel possibilities become invitations or "lures" for occasions to actualize themselves in particular ways.[24] In this way, God is both the *ground of infinite novelty* and the *principle of limitation*.[25]

In more explicitly theological terms, Cobb is claiming that God offers *Godself* as an invitation for every moment of becoming toward the aesthetic "enrichment of life, variety of forms, intensity of experience, consciousness, and love."[26] The divine lure is therefore nothing less than the sustaining, ordering, and enlivening presence of the Spirit throughout creation.[27] In this way, Cobb believes that God is always becoming incarnate in some measure throughout creation with every occasion's prehension of the divine lure. As Whitehead wrote, "The world lives by its incarnation of God in itself."[28]

It is also important to point out that when an occasion prehends the divine lure, it is free to align with it more or less. Thus Cobb believes that humans can experience the divine lure as a "call" to bring about a certain good in a situation, or to actualize a certain value in some moment: "God is the One Who Calls us beyond all that we have become to what we might be."[29] As the metaphor of a divine "call" suggests, even though the divine

---

22. Ibid., 99.
23. Whitehead, *Science and the Modern World*, 177.
24. Ibid., 53.
25. Ibid., 92.
26. Cobb, *Is It Too Late?*, 71.
27. Birch and Cobb, *The Liberation of Life*, 199.
28. Whitehead, *Religion In the Making*, 140.
29. Cobb, *God and the World*, 82.

lure is the initiating grace for every occasion, God *cannot* determine any outcome.[30] God is therefore omni-*potential* rather than omni-*potent*. Thus because God's creative power is *persuasive* rather than *coercive*, the divine "call" is often difficult for us to discern, lacking the magical clarity of divine dictation.

Additionally, God's inability to coerce, determine, or intervene in creation is not due to some kind of voluntary self-limitation to give creatures freedom. This has become increasingly common in Christian theology (as in the theology of Jürgen Moltmann, for example), but it is not Cobb's approach. Although there are important *metaphysical* reasons for Cobb's total rejection of omnipotence, the *theological* reason is that God's nature must be defined by love in a more radical sense than has often been recognized:

> Although the result of Jesus' message, life, and death should have been to redefine power in terms of the divine love, this did not happen. Power, in the sense of controlling domination, remained the *essential* definition of deity. . . . Process theology's understanding of divine love is in harmony with the insight, which we can gain both from psychologists and from our own experience, that if we truly love others we do not seek to control them.[31]

The God of the Bible who is essentially love rather than controlling power thus requires creaturely cooperation and positive responses to her call in order to accomplish her purposes. Through genuine mutuality rather than one-sided domination and force, God never intervenes unilaterally in order to determine events, according to Cobb. To do otherwise would involve a contradiction of God's nature as love. As such, God works patiently with every creaturely decision in order to bring about any value or good in creation. And because *everything* has some ability to respond in process thought, the lure of God is active throughout creation—not merely through conscious human minds. Cobb thus proposes a deeply ecological vision in which everything has some value and co-creative potential.

Thus far, I have shown how Cobb understands the creative action of God in the world. This is what he calls the *creative love* of God. However, he also argues that God is lovingly *responsive* to the world: experiencing its sufferings and joys and then redeeming each occasion within the divine life. As with Cobb's argument against an interventionist God, this claim goes against much of the Christian tradition that has often only affirmed

---

30. Cobb, *A Christian Natural Theology*, 246.
31. Cobb and Griffin, *Process Theology*, 53.

Apocalypse of Love

God's creative action and denied that God was in any way *moved* by the world.[32] Cobb holds to a more dynamic vision of God and the world that can be likened to the call-and-response musical patterns in jazz, gospel, blues and other types of improvisational music: God creatively acts in the world and the world responds; the world reacts upon God, who in turn responds. For Cobb, both the witness of the Bible as a whole and Jesus in particular define love for Christians in a way that must include a radical sense of empathy and mutuality.[33] If God's nature is truly defined by love, Cobb argues, then God must be seen as both creative *and* responsive love.

For Cobb, God is dipolar like all actualities.[34] As such, he explains that the divine has a mental pole, or primordial nature, which he associates with God's *creative love*; but there is also a divine physical pole, or consequent nature, which he associates with God's *responsive love*. To be sure, there are important differences between God and the world. First of all, God is not spatially limited but is equally everywhere: *with* and *in* everything, while not *being* everything (i.e., this is not pantheism).[35] God is also nontemporal in the sense that God does not perish into the past or experience loss in the same way as other actualities. Even so, Cobb argues that "time and history are real for God," whose being is "affected by temporal events" in a fully open, undecided future.[36] As the one nontemporal actual process, God everlastingly *creates* and *responds* to a world of occasions.

Bringing these multiple descriptions of the dynamic God-world interaction together, Cobb's process vision can be imagined as follows: God envisages and orders possibilities in her primordial nature with the aim of calling forth certain values in creation; every event in the world prehends other actualities, including God, as well as the possibilities that God offers as lures to bring forth values; God also lovingly responds to creation at every moment through her consequent nature; and finally, God's prehension of the world's multiplicities influences the dynamic ordering of infinite possibilities, thereby enabling God to offer possibilities of greater relevance for every new moment.[37] Cobb's theo-cosmology is thus a form of "panentheism": God and the world are distinct yet interdependent; God

---

32. Ibid., 45.
33. Cobb, *Christ in a Pluralistic Age*, 86.
34. Cobb, *A Christian Natural Theology*, 110.
35. Ibid., 157.
36. Ibid., 122, 158.
37. Ibid., 124.

is in the world yet the world is also in God; and God is both changing and unchanging in different respects.[38] How might Cobb's panentheistic God of creative-responsive love illuminate both the cultural significance and existential dimensions of the Beach Boys' *Pet Sounds*? It is to this question that I now turn.

Part II: The Creative Love of God and the Apocalypse of *Pet Sounds*

For many Christians, the arts are often viewed as a mere means to an end—a *secular* means to a *sacred* end. A great deal of so-called "Christian music" thus tends to be understood in this way: as little more than a time-bound tool to communicate the eternal truth of the gospel. The arts are then seen as instrumentally rather than intrinsically valuable, and even as a "lower" *material* thing as opposed to a "higher" *spiritual* truth. But this kind of dualistic world view, with the material and the secular sharply divided from the spiritual and the sacred, arguably impoverishes our appreciation for and engagement with the arts. Alternatively, perhaps we can begin to discern Christ as incarnate within creativity and the arts, as an immanent source of inspiration towards Beauty. Might we then learn to see great works of art like *Pet Sounds* as mysterious *disclosures of* Christ rather than as mere *means to* Christ—between which there is a constitutive relation rather than a chasm? Here one might think of Colossians 3:11, which asserts that Christ "is all, and in all." This notion is also beautifully echoed in a noncanonical saying of Jesus: "Split a piece of wood, I am there. Lift a stone, and you will find me there" (*Gospel of Thomas*, Logion 77).

Because of Cobb's vision of God's loving and gracious action in creation as an immanent lure towards Beauty—here understood as an aesthetic "harmony of contrasts"—I believe that his process theology can offer an inspiring perspective on the arts for Christians today.[39] Without simply *reducing* the sacred to the arts, Cobb's theo-cosmology allows us to see the sacred as always *enfolded within* the arts—although in varying intensities, to be sure. With this perspective in mind, far from being just an impressive aspect of secular twentieth-century culture, the beautiful and creative achievement of the Beach Boys' *Pet Sounds* might now be seen as an instance of the sacred within the secular—or an instance of "creative

---

38. Cobb, *God and the World*, 80.
39. Haught, *What Is Religion?*, 173.

Apocalypse of Love

transformation," as Cobb would name it. For in a process perspective of entangled becomings, the sacred and the secular are inseparable.

Cobb's powerful notion of creative transformation is, as I have already begun to suggest, a way of theologically interpreting the emergence of novel forms of Beauty within history and culture. It is a universal activity, although it is always radically contextual. And neither is it inevitable, for it depends upon many variables that God cannot control. As I tried to show in part one, Cobb argues that the movement of life is a process constituted by the past, God, and the agency of individual creatures. However, it is also an unpredictable process of change that can bring destruction just as much as it can bring creation and salvation for creatures.[40] While most of what we typically call "change" involves mere rearrangements and even rejections of the past, Cobb argues that God's aim is for the movement of creation toward novel forms of Beauty that *include* the past in new complexities: "The new builds upon the old and transfuses it with meaning it could not have apart from the new. The new not only frees us from the old but also frees us for it."[41]

Without God's gracious offering of the divine lure to every occasion, there would be no chance for creative transformation to take place in the world. Cobb understands all instances of creative transformation to occur through God's "introduction of novelties into experience so as to transform discordant elements of past experience into contrasts," harmoniously including them within a new creative becoming.[42] As the process of growth and life, creative transformation happens all the time, as aesthetically intense "instances of enlargement" that incorporate the past of a becoming occasion with new potentialities.[43]

This important soteriological notion of creative transformation is also crucial for Cobb's cosmic Logos Christology. In his classic book *Christ In a Pluralistic Age*, he argues that the primordial nature of God—the source of her creative love—should be understood as the eternal Word or Logos of John 1. As the "the cosmic principle of order, the ground of meaning, and the source of purpose," Christians can affirm that the divine Logos was fully incarnate in Jesus of Nazareth, according to Cobb.[44] Although he cer-

---

40. Coleman, *Making a Way Out of No Way*, 86.
41. Cobb, *Christ in a Pluralistic Age*, 59–60.
42. Bube, *Ethics in John Cobb's Process Theology*, 69.
43. Bowman and McDaniel, *Handbook of Process Theology*, 33–34.
44. Cobb, *Christ in a Pluralistic Age*, 71.

tainly affirms God's presence within all things, Cobb also believes that God was uniquely present in Jesus in the sense that his self was co-constituted by the prehension of his past and of God. Unlike other humans, Jesus did not experience God as "other" because there was no tension between his particular moment-by-moment aims and the divine lure. This was due to Jesus' faithful responses to God's call for his creative-aesthetic becomings throughout his life.[45] Cobb can thus affirm, in his own particular way, that Jesus was "truly God and truly human."[46] While genuinely human in every way, Cobb believes that Jesus was also "God's decisive revelation" of creative-responsive love.[47]

Therefore, *as incarnate*, the cosmic Logos can be identified with Christ. As such, Cobb argues that Christ is to be discerned as creatively present in all things: "the universal principle of life and light, creation and redemption, which is the presence of God in all things . . . the redemptive, creative activity of God everywhere . . . ."[48] However, Christ is not *equally* within everything, but "is present to a greater or lesser extent as creatures freely decide for or against the Logos."[49] One can discern Christ anywhere that events of creative transformation seem to occur: in individuals, religions, science, politics, theology, and the arts.[50] But Christ is always salvifically at work in the world—recognized or not. And even though Cobb argues that the effectiveness of creative transformation in the world can potentially be increased when communities do recognize Jesus as truly *the* Christ, it is not necessary for this to be acknowledged for events of creative transformation to occur. Indeed, Cobb believes that the creative love of God in Christ has been graciously at work throughout history in many diverse persons who do not confess Jesus as the Christ.

As such, regardless of any artist's particular faith, the lure of God can still inspire Beauty in their work and disclose redemptive possibilities in surprising places. For Christians, Christ might therefore be discerned in music that lacks any obvious reference to Jesus, such as the Beach Boys' *Pet Sounds*. And who would doubt that this revolutionary album is anything but an instance of creative transformation, with its brilliant fusion of

---

45. Ibid., 139–140.
46. Cobb, *The Process Perspective*, 45.
47. Cobb and Griffin, *Process Theology*, 105.
48. Cobb, *The Process Perspective*, 37.
49. Cobb and Griffin, *Process Theology*, 99.
50. Cobb, *Christ in a Pluralistic Age*, 87.

unusual instruments, layered vocals, and found sounds? Indeed, it would seem to exemplify Cobb's sense of Beauty as an aesthetic harmony of contrasts. Within their context, the Beach Boys creatively built upon many of the greatest musical achievements of the past and produced something genuinely new and beautiful in the history of music. Before the album was released, few could have imagined such a complex and novel musical synthesis that would become so influential for Western music. By drawing on Cobb's process theology, Christians might therefore welcome this kind of "secular" apocalypse of love, and others like it, as disclosures of Christ's ongoing creative work within culture. The sacred and the secular *enfolded*, indeed.

Part III: The Responsive Love of God and Perpetual Perishing in *Pet Sounds*

But what happens when things begin to *unfold*—when events of all kinds inevitably escape our grasp and drift further and further away from every present? Do they finally perish into the past as ever-diminishing influences upon new becomings, and thus ultimately dissolving into nothingness or disappearing within a great cosmic void? Indeed, our inescapable sense of radical contingency and transience in the world might ultimately cause some of us to wonder about the final value and meaning of *anything* in history. It was perhaps Nietzsche who most famously expressed this possible threat of nihilism: "In some remote corner of the universe, poured out and glittering in innumerable solar systems, there once was a star on which clever animals invented knowledge . . . . After nature had drawn a few breaths the star grew cold, and the clever animals had to die."[51] In the face of our perpetual perishing, radical contingency, and the inevitability of death—so powerfully recognized by Nietzsche and other existentialists—what grounds are there for courage and hope? Might we somehow imagine new beginnings, or even new life? This brings me to a final consideration of process and *Pet Sounds*, which is appropriately eschatological.

One of the most intriguing lyrical themes throughout *Pet Sounds* is the struggle over the loss of youth, with its subtle reflections on the inevitably fading moments of joy and love that we often desire to relive or somehow sustain. These anxieties are expressed in a number of songs on *Pet Sounds*, such as "Caroline, No" that speaks of a hope to recover lost moments of

---

51. Nietzsche, *The Portable Nietzsche*, 42.

bliss between two lovers: "Could we ever bring them back once they have gone?" For the lyricists Brian Wilson and Tony Asher, having to see such "a sweet thing die" is a tragic but seemingly inevitable experience. Another striking example of this theme is found on the song "Here Today." After expressing a great sense of wonder and excitement about newfound love, Asher cautions, "Love is here today and it's gone tomorrow." Without exception, they seem to suggest, every experience of love perishes "so fast."[52]

Taking these existential reflections as my starting point, what I want to explore in this final section of the chapter is how Cobb's theological notion of God's responsive love can facilitate a humble but genuine sense of confidence in the intrinsic value of these always fleeting moments. In spite of the fact that every value, experience, and accomplishment slowly but surely fades into the past, the responsive love of God provides us with the grounds for hope that there is nevertheless enduring importance for every instance of truth, Beauty, and goodness—that in the end, every micro-apocalypse of love everlastingly *matters* to God. Cobb's explanation of this claim is based on Whitehead's view that God "saves the world as it passes into the immediacy of his own life."[53]

As we have seen, Cobb attempts to ground his understanding of God on the basis of love, such that the divine is both creative *in* the world and responsive *to* the world. The responsive love of God is thus understood as divine empathy, or the ability to be *affected* by the pains and the joys of every single occasion of experience. This follows from the claim that God is, like everything else, an actuality who aesthetically prehends the multiplicity of other actualities. As such, whatever happens in the world immediately passes into the experience of God's own life as a constitutive influence. In the process of God's own everlasting becoming, every event is saved and transformed—one could even say *resurrected*—into the divine life.

Cobb believes that God lovingly finds a way to save *every* perished occasion, and not merely events of love, joy, or Beauty. Each occasion is to some degree transformed by God while dynamically integrated into an "everlasting and growing harmony" within the divine consequent nature.[54] This always fragile, incomplete, but nevertheless salvific divine reality corresponds to the biblical kingdom of heaven—or what Cobb prefers to call the "Commonwealth of God"—that every occasion contributes to in some

52. The Beach Boys, *Pet Sounds*.
53. Whitehead, *Process and Reality*, 343.
54. Cobb, *Christ in a Pluralistic Age*, 226.

Apocalypse of Love

way. But even though God does find a way for everything to participate in the divine Commonwealth, God's own aesthetic experience is enriched or impoverished depending on the quality of our contributions. God knows the greater good that we *could* have chosen and experiences the good that we *do* sometimes choose.

For Cobb, it is thus precisely because events in the world really *affect* God's own experience that we have grounds for hope in the face of perpetual perishing. By forever saving every occasion in its full immediacy and value within God's consequent nature, the responsive love of God provides the world with objective immortality.[55] In this way, Cobb argues, God is the ground of meaning, and therefore releases us from the anxiety of perpetual perishing: that inescapable fact that past occasions fade into triviality, and along with them, historical events of truth, beauty, and goodness.[56] In the end, Cobb believes that life would be meaningless without this sense of God's responsive love:

> the divine experience is not something outside and self-contained. Instead it is constituted by the creative unification of all the creaturely experiences. In the world these fade, losing their immediacy and distinctive value. In the divine experience they remain forever in their immediacy and in the fullness of their particular value . . . . To know ourselves as forever alive in God, provides us the context of meaning within which the ephemeral finitude of life can be celebrated and the penultimate importance of history understood and lived.[57]

Through these endless resurrections of the world into God, we can fully affirm life, love, and meaning, Cobb argues. We can know that the last word for creation is not the tragedy of perpetual perishing. In Cobb's process-relational cosmology, we never merely unfold into a fading past but into the divine life as well—and hence, God enfolds *us*. Accordingly, while it is true that a great musical apocalypse like *Pet Sounds* will slowly decline in importance over time, Cobb's process vision helps us understand that such a work of remarkable Beauty has forever influenced God's own aesthetic becoming. For God does not just provoke Beauty—she *enjoys* it. But this divine enjoyment of creation is not the end of the story. In this vision, the fragile Beauty of creation that endlessly swirls back into God's reconciling

---

55. Cobb, *A Christian Natural Theology*, 128.
56. Cobb and Griffin, *Process Theology*, 120.
57. Cobb, "The Resurrection of the Soul," 226–27.

life in turn "floods back again into the world," transformed as divine love for new aesthetic becomings.[58]

Along with the fleeting moments of youthful love that the Beach Boys struggled to come to terms with, their musical incarnation of Beauty everlastingly matters to God as an instance of creative transformation, a micro-apocalypse of love, along with many others that are continuously being woven into the divine Commonwealth. Might we therefore imagine Christ as immanently present in our creative activities, as collaborating with us in our productive occasions of Beauty, which in turn fold into God's enjoyment and unfold back as the love of creative becomings? This is a truly cosmic vision of creativity that can, perhaps, inspire Christians to embrace the arts with renewed passion and engagement. For in this relational musicosmology, the divine is like a poet or a musician who lovingly invites and creatively responds to our endlessly becoming world—arranging verse, layering sound—into an always multiplying instance of Beauty: the eschatological peace of a "Harmony of Harmonies."[59]

---

58. Whitehead, *Process and Reality*, 351.
59. Whitehead, *Adventures of Ideas*, 296.

Bibliography

"The 100 Greatest Albums Ever Made." *Mojo*, August 1995. http://www.freerepublic.com/focus/chat/694838/posts.

"500 Greatest Albums of All Time: The Beach Boys, 'Pet Sounds.'" *Rolling Stone*. http://www.rollingstone.com/music/lists/500-greatest-albums-of-all-time-20120531/the-beach-boys-pet-sounds-20120524.

Abbott, Kingsley. *The Beach Boys' Pet Sounds: The Greatest Album of the Twentieth Century*. London: Helter Skelter, 2001.

Altenmüller, Eckart, et al. "Neural Reorganization Underlies Improvement in Stroke-Induced Motor Dysfunction by Music-Supported Therapy." *Annals of the New York Academy of Sciences* 1169 (2009) 395–405.

Anselm. "Proslogion." In *Anselm of Canterbury: The Major Works*, translated and edited by Brian Davies and G. R. Evans, 82–104. Oxford: Oxford University Press, 1998.

Aquinas, St. Thomas. *Treatise on the Virtues*. Translated by John A. Oesterle. Notre Dame, IN: University of Notre Dame Press, 1984.

Augustine. *Expositions of the Psalms*. Translated by Maria Boulding. Hyde Park, NY: New City, 2003.

———. *Later Works*. Philadelphia: Westminster, 1955.

Badman, Keith. *The Beach Boys: The Definitive Diary of America's Greatest Band on Stage and in the Studio*. Montclair, NJ: Backbeat, 2004.

Bagge, Peter. *Hate*. Annual no. 2. Seattle: Fantagraphics, 2002.

Barth, Karl. *Dogmatics in Outline*. Translated by G. T. Thompson. New York: Philosophical Library, 1949.

The Beach Boys: An American Band? Brian Wilson: I Just Wasn't Made for These Times. DVD. Directed by Malcolm Leo and Don Was. High Ridge Productions, 1985.

The Beach Boys. *Good Vibrations*. Liner notes booklet. Capitol Records, .

———. *Pet Sounds*. Liner notes by Mark Linnet, Brian Wilson, and David Leaf. Capitol Records, 1990.

———. *Pet Sounds*. Capitol Records, 1966.

———. *The Pet Sounds Sessions*. Liner notes booklet. Capitol Records, 1996.

———. *SMiLE Sessions*. Capitol Records, 2001.

Beck, Melinda. "A Key for Unlocking Memories." *The Wall Street Journal*, November 17, 2009, D1–2.

Bell, Daniel. *Economy of Desire: Christianity and Capitalism in a Postmodern World*. Grand Rapids: Baker Academic, 2012.

Bibliography

Birch, Charles, and John B. Cobb. *The Liberation of Life: From the Cell to the Community.* Denton, TX: Environmental Ethics, 1990.

Bower, Bruce. "Birth of the Beat." *Science News* 178, no. 4 (2010) 18–23.

Bowman, Donna, and Jay McDaniel. *Handbook of Process Theology.* St. Louis: Chalice, 2006.

Bradshaw, D. H., et al. "Individual Differences in the Effects of Music Engagement on Responses to Painful Stimulation." *Journal of Pain* 12, no. 12 (2011) 1262–73.

Brantley, Jeffrey. *Calming Your Anxious Mind.* Oakland, CA: New Harbinger, 2007.

Boyd, Alan. "Producer's Notes." *The SMiLE Sessions.* Liner notes. Capitol Records, 2001.

Brockris, Vic. *Keith Richards: The Biography.* London: Penguin, 1992.

Brueggemann, Walter. *Sabbath as Resistance: Saying No to the Culture of Now.* Louisville: Westminster John Knox, 2014.

Bube, Paul D. *Ethics in John Cobb's Process Theology.* Atlanta: Scholars, 1988.

Calvin, John. *Institutes of the Christian Religion.* Peabody, MA: Hendrickson, 2009.

Caputo, John D. *The Insistence of God: A Theology of Perhaps.* Bloomington, IN: Indiana University Press, 2013.

Carlin, Peter Ames. *Catch a Wave: The Rise, Fall, and Redemption of the Beach Boys' Brian Wilson.* Emmaus, PA: Rodale, 2006.

Catholic Church. *Catechism of the Catholic Church*, 2nd ed. New York: Doubleday, 1995.

Cobb, John B. *A Christian Natural Theology: Based on the Thought of Alfred North Whitehead.* 2nd ed. Louisville: Westminster John Knox, 2007.

———. *Christ in a Pluralistic Age.* Eugene, OR: Wipf and Stock, 1999.

———. *The Earthist Challenge to Economism.* London: Palgrave Macmillan, 1998.

———. *God and the World.* Eugene, OR: Wipf and Stock, 1998.

———. *Is It Too Late?: A Theology of Ecology.* Denton, TX: Environmental Ethics, 1995.

———. *The Process Perspective: Frequently Asked Questions about Process Theology.* Edited by Jeanyne B. Slettom. St. Louis: Chalice, 2003.

———. "The Resurrection of the Soul." *Harvard Theological Review* 80, no. 2 (March 2, 1987) 213–27.

Cobb, John B., and David Ray Griffin. *Process Theology: An Introductory Exposition.* Philadelphia: Westminster, 1976.

Cody, John. "Brian Wilson, The Beach Boys' Musical Genius." *Johncodyonline*, 2002. http://www.johncodyonline.com/home/articles/2002-11-brianwilson.

Coleman, Monica A. *Making a Way Out of No Way: A Womanist Theology.* Minneapolis: Fortress, 2008.

Cooper, Chet. "Brian Wilson—a Powerful Interview." *Ability*, 2006, 45–53.

Cranmer, Thomas. "The Prayer of Dr. Cranmer, Archbishop." In *The Remains*, 136–42. London: Oxford University Press, 1833.

DeCurtis, Anthony. Interview from *Brian Wilson: Songwriter 1962–1969.* DVD Chrome, 2010.

DeRogatis, Jim. *Milk It!: Collected Musings On the Alternative Music Explosion of the 90s.* Cambridge, MA: Da Capo, 2003.

Dillenberger, John. "Faith." In *A New Handbook of Christian Theology*, edited by Donald W. Musser and Joseph L. Price. Nashville: Abingdon, 1996. Ministry Matters Online Database. http://www.ministrymatters.com/library/#/abdict42/c80e5376a64e7411be9fb4277b7f478d/faith.html.

DiMartino, Dave. "Give Radiohead Your Computer." *myLaunch*, May 2, 1998. http://www.followmearound.com/presscuttings.php?year=1998&cutting=60.

Bibliography

Dorrien, Gary. "David Griffin's Whiteheadian Religious Philosophy." *Reason & Reenchantment: The Philosophical, Religious, and Political Thought of David Ray Griffin*. Edited by John B. Cobb, Richard A. Falk, and Catherine Keller, 15–32. Claremont, CA: Process Century, 2013.

———. "Dialectics of Difference: Barth, Whitehead, Modern Theology and the Uses of Worldviews." *American Journal of Theology & Philosophy*, 30, no. 3 (September 2009) 244–70.

———. "The Lure and Necessity of Process Theology." *CrossCurrents*, 58 (2008) 316–36.

Eippert, Falk, et al. "Direct Evidence for Spinal Cord Involvement in Placebo Analgesia." *Science News* 326, no. 5951 (2009) 404.

Emerson, Ralph Waldo. "The Conservative." 1841. *Ralph Waldo Emerson Texts*. http://www.emersoncentral.com/conservative.htm.

———. "Nature." 1836. *Ralph Waldo Emerson Texts*. http://www.emersoncentral.com/nature1.htm.

———. "The Poet." 1844. *Ralph Waldo Emerson Texts*. http://www.emersoncentral.com/poet.htm.

———. "Self-Reliance." 1841. *Ralph Waldo Emerson Texts*. http://www.emersoncentral.com/selfreliance.htm.

Epstein, Lawrence J. *Political Folk Music in America from Its Origins to Bob Dylan*. Jefferson, NC: McFarland & Company, 2010.

Fischer, John. "In Brian Wilson's Room." January 26, 2007. https://www.breakpoint.org/features-columns/articles/entry/12/9440.

Forde, Gerhard. *On Being a Theologian of the Cross*. Grand Rapids: Eerdmans, 1997.

———. *Where God Meets Man: A Down-to-Earth Approach to the Gospel*. Minneapolis: Augsburg, 1977.

Fusilli, Jim. *Pet Sounds: 33 1/3*. New York: Continuum, 2005.

Gaidos, Susan. "More Than a Feeling." *Science News* 178, no. 4 (2010) 24–29.

Gaines, Steven. *Heroes and Villains: The True Story of The Beach Boys*. New York: Signet, 1986.

———. *Heroes and Villains: The True Story of the Beach Boys*. New York: Nal, 1986.

Granata, Charles L. *Wouldn't It Be Nice: Brian Wilson and the Making of the Beach Boys' Pet Sounds*. Chicago: Chicago Review, 2003.

Groopman, Jerome. *The Anatomy of Hope: How People Prevail in the Face of Illness*. New York: Random House, 2004.

———. "The Biology of Hope." *Acumen Journal of Life Sciences* II, no. 1 (2004) 55–61.

Guinn, Jeff. *Manson: The Life and Times of Charles Manson*. New York: Simon and Schuster, 2014.

Harrison, Daniel. "After Sundown: The Beach Boys' Experimental Music." In *Understanding Rock: Essays in Musical Analysis*, edited by John Covach and Graeme M. Boone, 33–58. New York: Oxford University Press, 1997.

Hatfield, Elaine, et al. *Emotional Contagion*. Cambridge: Cambridge University Press, 1994.

Haught, John F. *What Is Religion?: An Introduction*. Mahwah, NJ: Paulist, 1990.

Heidegger, Martin. "The Origin of the Work of Art." In *Poetry, Language, Thought*, translated by Albert Hofstadter, 15–86. New York: Harper and Row, 1971.

———. "What Are Poets For?" In *Poetry, Language, Thought*, translated by Albert Hofstadter, 87–140. New York: Harper and Row, 1971.

Heschel, Abraham J. *The Sabbath*. New York: Farrar, Straus and Giroux, 2005.

Bibliography

Huxley, Aldous. *The Doors of Perception*. New York: Harper and Brothers, 1954.

James, William. *Varieties of Religious Experience*. Lecture VIII: "The Divided Self, and the Process of its Unification." http://xroads.virginia.edu/~Hyper/WJAMES/. Lectures VI & VII: http://csp.org/experience/james-varieties/james-varieties6.html.

Janata, Petr. "The Neural Architecture of Music-Evoked Autobiographical Memories." *Cerebral Cortex* 19, no. 11 (2009) 2579–94.

Juslin, Patrick N. "Communicating Emotion in Music Performance: A Review and a Theoretical Framework." In *Music and Emotion: Theory and Research*, edited by Patrick N. Juslin and John A. Sloboda, 309–37. Oxford: Oxford University Press, 2001.

Juslin, Patrick N., and John Sloboda, eds. *Handbook of Music and Emotion: Theory, Research, Applications*. New York: Oxford University Press, 2010.

Juslin, Patrick N., and Daniel Västifäll. "Emotional Responses to Music: The Need to Consider Underlying Mechanisms." *Behavioral and Brain Sciences* 31 (2008) 559–621.

Kant, Immanuel. *An Answer to the Question: "What is Enlightenment?"* Translated by H. B. Nisbet. London: Penguin, 2009.

Keller, Catherine. *Apocalypse Now and Then*. Minneapolis: Augsburg Fortress, 1996.

Kent, Nick. *The Dark Stuff: Selected Writings on Rock Music*. New York: Da Capo, 2002, 2009.

Kierkegaard, Soren. *Either/Or*. Edited by H. V. Hong. Princeton, NJ: Princeton University Press, 1987.

———. *The Stages on Life's Way*. Edited by H. V. Hong. Princeton, NJ: Princeton University Press, 1988.

———. *Works of Love*. New York: HarperPerennial, 2009.

———. *Works of Love*. New York: Harper-Collins, 2009.

Koelsch, Stefan. "Towards a Neural Basis of Music-Evoked Emotions." *Trends in Cognitive Sciences* 14, no. 3 (2010) 101–46.

Kreider, Tim. "I Know What You Think of Me." *New York Times* Opinion Pages, June 15, 2013. www.opinionator.blogs.nytimes.com/2013/06/15/i-know-what-you-think-of-me.

Lambert, Philip. *Inside the Music of Brian Wilson: The Songs, Sounds and Influences of the Beach Boys' Founding Genius*. New York: Continuum, 2007.

Leaf, David. *The Beach Boys and the California Myth*. New York: Grosset and Dunlap, 1978.

———. *Beautiful Dreamer: Brian Wilson and the Story of Smile*, DVD. Chautauqua Entertainment, 2004.

Leary, Timothy. *The Psychedelic Experience*. Kensington, NY: Citadel, 1964.

Levitin, Daniel J. *This Is Your Brain on Music: The Science of a Human Obsession*. New York: Dutton, 2006.

Levitin, Daniel J., and Anna K. Tirovolas. "Current Advances in the Cognitive Neurosciences of Music." *Annals of the New York Academy of Sciences* 1156 (2009) 211–31.

Luther, Martin. *Luther's Works*, vol. 14. Edited by Jaroslav Pelikan and Daniel E. Poellott. Translated by Arnold Guebert. St. Louis: Concordia, 1958.

The Making of Pet Sounds. Booklet accompanying *The Beach Boys: The Pet Sounds Sessions*. Capitol, 1996.

Bibliography

Manon, Hugh S. "The Jouissance of Jargon." *World Picture 1*, Spring 2008. http://www.worldpicturejournal.com/World%20Picture/WP_1.1/Manon.pdf.

Maples, Wendy. "Surf culture." July 19, 2010. http://www.open.edu/openlearn/body-mind/health/sport-and-fitness/sport/surf-culture.

Marcel, Gabriel. *Creative Fidelity*. New York: Fordham University Press, 2002.

———. *The Mystery of Being, Volume II: Faith and Reality*. South Bend, IN: Saint Augustine's, 2001.

———. *Music and Philosophy*. Translated by Stephen Maddux and Robert E. Wood. Milwaukee: Marquette University Press, 2005.

Martin, Bill. *Listening to the Future: The Time of Progressive Rock*. Chicago: Open Court, 1998.

Merleau-Ponty, Maurice. *The World of Perception*. New York: Routledge, 2002.

———. *Sense and Non-Sense*. Evanston, IL: Northwestern University Press, 1964.

———. *Phenomenology of Perception*. New York: Routledge, 2002.

Miller, Jim. "The Beach Boys." In *The Rolling Stone Illustrated History of Rock and Roll: The Definitive History of the Most Important Artists and Their Music*, edited by Anthony DeCurtis, James Henke, and Holly George-Warren, 192–99. New York: Random House, 1992.

Moltmann, Jürgen. *Theology and Joy*. London: SCM, 1973.

Mora, Meike Shedden, et al. "Lessons Learned from Placebo Groups in Antidepressant Trials." *Philosophical Transactions of the Royal Society B: Biological Sciences* 366, no. 1572 (2011) 1879–88.

Neuman, R., and F. Strack. "Mood Contagion: The Automatic Transfer of Mood between Persons." *Journal of Personality and Social Psychology* 79 (2000) 211–23.

Kent, Nick. "The Last Beach Movie Revisited: The Life of Brian Wilson." In *The Dark Stuff: Selected Writings on Rock Music*, 1–74. Cambridge, MA: Da Capo, 2002.

Nietzsche, Friedrich. *The Portable Nietzsche*. Edited by Walter Kaufmann. London: Penguin, 1977.

Nilsson, S., et al. "School-Aged Children's Experiences of Postoperative Music Medicine on Pain, Distress, and Anxiety." *Paediatr Anaesthia* 19, no. 12 (2009) 1184–90.

O'Hagan, Sean. "A Boy's Own Story." *The Observer*, January 5, 2002. http://www.theguardian.com/theobserver/2002/jan/06/features.review87.

Osborne, John W. "The Mapping of Thoughts, Emotions, Sensations, and Images as Responses to Music." *Journal of Mental Imagery* 5, no. 1 (1981) 133–36.

Petridis, Alexis. "The Astonishing Genius of Brian Wilson." *The Guardian*, June 24, 2011. http://www.theguardian.com/music/2011/jun/24/brian-wilson-interview.

Pieper, Joseph. *Faith, Hope, Love*. San Francisco: Ignatius, 1997.

Pinker, Steven. "Less Faith, More Reason." *The Harvard Crimson*, October 27, 2006. http://www.thecrimson.com/article/2006/10/27/less-faith-more-reason-there-is/.

Plutchik, Robert. "Emotions and Imagery." *Journal of Mental Imagery* 8, no. 4 (1984) 105–11.

Priore, Domenic. *Look! Listen! Vibrate! Smile!* San Francisco: Fourth Last Gasp, 1995.

Reum, Peter. "Lost and Found: The Significance of SMiLE." Liner notes to *The SMiLE Sessions*. Capitol Records, 2001.

Roholt, Tiger. "In Praise of Ambiguity: Musical Subtlety and Merleau-Ponty." http://www.contempaesthetics.org/newvolume/pages/article.php?articleID=669.

Sanchez, Luis. *The Beach Boys' Smile*. New York: Bloomsbury, 2014.

Bibliography

Schott, Ben. "Oversouling." *New York Times*, February 14, 2011. http://schott.blogs.nytimes.com/2011/02/14/oversouling/?_php=true&_type=blogs&ref=jerrywexler&_r=0.

Serong, Jock. "There is a god, and she wants us to surf." December 3, 2013. http://www.theguardian.com/commentisfree/2013/dec/04/surfing-spirituality.

Siegel, Jules. "Goodbye Surfing, Hello God!" *The Atavist*, 8 (October/November 2011). Kindle electronic edition.

———. *Goodbye Surfing, Hello God! The Atavist*, 2011. https://atavist.com/stories/goodbye-surfing-hello-god/.

———. "Goodbye Surfing, Hello God: Brian Wilson's Tortured Effort to Finish 'Smile.'" *Rolling Stone*, November, 2011. http://www.rollingstone.com/music/news/goodbye-surfing-hello-god-brian-wilsons-tortured-effort-to-finish-smile-20111103.

SMiLE. Liner notes. Capitol Records, 2001.

Society for Neuroscience. "Feelings of Hope Create Striking Brain Effects That Could Help Alleviate Serious Afflictions Like Pain, Parkinson's Disease, and Depression, Researchers Report." http://www.sfn.org/Press-Room/News-Release-Archives/2005/FEELINGS-OF-HOPE.

Specter, Michael. "The Power of Nothing." *The New Yorker* 87, no. 40 (2011) 30–36.

Stevens, Robert. "An Evening with Brian Wilson." *World Socialist Web Site*. October 24, 2007. https://www5.wsws.org/development/en/articles/2007/10/wils-024.html?view=print.

Taylor, Charles. *A Secular Age*. Cambridge, MA: Harvard University Press, 2007.

Taylor, Mark L. *The Theological and the Political: On the Weight of the World*. Minneapolis: Fortress, 2011.

"This is Your Brain on Jazz: Researchers Use MRI to Study Spontaneity, Creativity." Press release, February 26, 2008. http://www.hopkinsmedicine.org/news/media/releases/this_is_your_brain_on_jazz_researchers_use_mri_to_study_spontaneity_creativity.

Tillich, Paul. *The Courage to Be*. New Haven, CT: Yale University Press, 1952.

———. *Theology of Culture*. Edited by Robert C. Kimball. Oxford: Oxford University Press, 1959.

Tomaino, Concetta. "Music Therapy for Neurological Conditions." PBS, May 21, 2009. Online interview: http://www.pbs.org/wnet/musicinstinct/video/music-and-medicine/music-therapy-for-neurological-conditions/72/.

"Tony Asher Interview." *Cabin Essence: Web Page for Brian Wilson*. April 4, 1996. http://www.surfermoon.com/interviews/asher.html.

Tutu, Desmond. "10 Questions for Desmond Tutu." *Time*, 175, no. 11, March 22, 2010, 4.

———. "Desmond Tutu Interview." Academy of Achievement, Chicago, June 12, 2004. http://www.achievement.org/autodoc/page/tutoint-1.

Ward, Ed. *A Nostalgic—But Bumpy—Journey with the Beach Boys*. December 10, 2013. http://www.npr.org/2013/12/10/249967933/a-nostalgic-yet-tainted-journey-with-the-beach-boys.

Watson, Alison, et al. "Placebo Conditioning and Placebo Analgesia Modulate a Common Brain Network During Pain Anticipation and Perception." *Pain* 145, no. 1–2 (2009) 24–30.

White, Timothy. *The Nearest Faraway Place: Brian Wilson, The Beach Boys, and the Southern California Experience*. New York: Henry Holt and Company, 1994.

———. *Sunflower/Surf's Up*. "Brothers-In-Arms: The Pioneering Road to Sunflower and 'Surf's Up.'" Liner notes to *SMiLe*. Capitol Records, 2001.

Bibliography

Whitehead, Alfred North. *Adventures of Ideas*. New York: Free Press, 1933.

———. *Process and Reality: An Essay In Cosmology*. Corrected ed. Gifford Lectures: 1927–1928. New York: Free Press, 1929.

———. *Religion In the Making*. New York: Fordham University Press, 1996.

———. *Science and the Modern World*. New York: Free Press, 1925.

Williams, Paul. *Brian Wilson and the Beach Boys: How Deep is the Ocean?* London: Omnibus, 2003.

Wilson, Brian. "Music is God's Voice." The Beach Boys, *The SMiLE Sessions* liner notes. Capitol Records, 2011.

Wilson, Brian, with Todd Gold. *Wouldn't It Be Nice? My Own Story*. New York: HarperCollins, 1991.

———. *Wouldn't It Be Nice? My Own Story*. London: Bloomsbury, 1996.

Wilson, Carl. "The Beach Boys—The Lord's Prayer." http://www.youtube.com/watch?v=HAobf3f9FQM.

Wiman, Christian. *My Bright Abyss: Meditations of a Modern Believer*. New York: MacMillan, 2013.

Wordsworth, William. "The Rainbow." In *The Poetical Works of William Wordsworth*, vol. II, edited by William Knight, 292. New York: Macmillan and Co., 1896.

Zahl, Paul. *Grace in Practice*. Grand Rapids: Eerdmans, 2007.

Zagorski, Nick. "The Science of Improv." *Peabody Magazine*, Fall 2008. http://www.peabody.jhu.edu/past_issues/fall08/the_science_of_improv.html

Zizek, Slavoj. *The Parallax View*. Cambridge, MA: MIT Press, 2006.

Zubieta, Jon-Kar, et al. "Placebo Effects Mediated by Endogenous Opioid Activity on Opioid Receptors." *The Journal of Neuroscience* 25, no. 34 (2005) 7754–62.

Index

Abbot, Kingsley, 41
abstraction, mistaken for concrete reality, 131
abuse, of the Wilson brothers, 6, 89
abyss
    Brian Wilson's encounter with, 51, 55, 58, 60
    experienced with existential eyes open, 54
    humans coming face to face with nonbeing, 53
"acceptance," renegotiating terms of, 104
"acceptance-in-spite-of," knowing about, 64
"accidental properties," sharing in an essence, 118
acoustic patterns, in music, 71
actual occasions, 130, 132
Adam and Eve, shame of exposure, 97
"Add Some Music," 113, 119–20
Add Some Music album, 111
aesthetic experiences
    as active, 112
    God's own, 141
aesthetic wholeness, Brian Wilson's quest for, 32–34
albums, sales of versus singles, 28
alienation, supreme statement of, 44
"All I Wanna Do," 113, 120–21
"All Summer Long," 79
All Summer Long, Beach Boys Concert, 29
allegiance, of an individual, 46
AllMusic online music site, 72

aloneness, humanity experiencing, 53
Alzheimer's patients, remembering song lyrics, 72
The Anatomy of Hope: How People Prevail in the Face of Illness (Groopman), 74
anger, 116
another person, as a spirit haunting a body, 115
Anselm, 18
anxiety
    of Brian Wilson, 27–28
    existential, 62
    of a finite being, 56
    kinds of, 86
    of perpetual perishing, 141
apocalypse of love, 139
apocalyptic disclosures, 128, 129
appearance, as reality, 123
Aquinas, St. Thomas, 68
art
    outsizing Brian Wilson's learning and taste, 99
    revealed through details, 118
    as secular means to a sacred end, 136
    self as focus of great, 46
artistic creativity, 19
artists
    Heidegger's hazardous role for, 53
    service to humanity, 52
    willing to go to the abyss, 53–54
Asher, Tony, 6, 14, 31, 35, 36, 41–42, 45, 99, 140
assassination, of John F. Kennedy, 89
auditory cortex, 69–70

Index

auditory form, writing or reading about, 7
Augustine, St., 25, 106
autism, music therapy treating, 72
autonomy, according to Kant, 12
aversion, to vulnerability, 97

Bagge, Peter, 98
Balzac, mystery of history, 112
"Barbara Ann," 30
Barth, Karl, 20, 21, 22
"Be My Baby," aping, 98
"Be True to Your School," 37, 80
Beach Boys
   argument against easy reading of music of, 6
   being too simplistic, 5
   compared to John Cobb, 128
   creative control for, 30
   during the early to mid-sixties, 78
   enlightened music of, 82
   harmonies and lyrics of, 77–80
   hippie and countercultural movements and, 83
   history of, 1
   hope and, 67, 68
   music analyzing something that must be experienced, 119
   music as therapeutic, 68, 81
   musical incarnation of Beauty, 142
   opinions on *Pet Sounds*, 34–35
   personal problems counterbalanced sweet vocal harmonies, 50
   Pet Sounds as most important album, 126–27
   pop culture lifestyle of, 87
   remaining endlessly fascinating, 95
   SMiLE, making available tapes of, 107
   "spiritual" side of their music, 2
   stereotype of California in the 1960s and, 87
   study in contradictions, 95
   surf culture and, 84
The Beach Boys' Christmas Album, 29
Beach Boys party album, 29
"beach" or "surf" sound, created by Beach Boys, 84

Beatles
   album as religious, 9
   competition with, 28, 105
   retirement from touring, 48–49
Beautiful Dreamer: Brian Wilson and the Story of "Smile," 52n5
Beauty
   as an aesthetic harmony of contrasts, 139
   of creation, 141–42
   within history and culture, 137
beauty, fashioning from ashes, 54
becoming, relational process of, 131
being, "in-spite-of," 61
believing, reason for, 14
Berry, Chuck, 79
Best of the Beach Boys, 46
bicycle bell, 39
Billings, William, 71
Blaine, Hal, 41
blindness, about the darker truths of life, 90
bliss, in the now, 86
body
   another person as a spirit haunting a, 115
   connection between the life of the mind and, 114
   with a history, 117
   inexplicably bound up with thought, 116
   mind and, 112, 131
   negative suggestions affecting, 75
Boyd, Alan, 15
brain regions, affected by improvisation, 19
"Bread and Wine," Hölderlin's elegy and, 52
"Break Away," 110
Bringing It All Back Home album (Dylan), 28
Britz, Chuck, 31
Brown, Bruce, 83
Brueggemann, Walter, 85n10
building up, as characteristic of love, 124–25
"Busy Doin' Nothing," 100

Index

"Cabinessence," 107
"California Girls," 29, 80
calm, from tiredness and worry, 121
Calvin, John, 13
Capitol Records, 29, 35–36
"Caroline, I know," 45
"Caroline No," 37, 38, 45, 104, 139–40
cars, 79–80
"Catch a Wave," 67, 79
The Catechism of the Catholic Church, on faith, 10–11
celestial tones, from Brian Wilson, 50
Cezanne, 111
"chatter," everyday, 119
child
  becoming, 26
  as the father of the man, 24, 108
  set free to play, 22
"Child is the Father of the Man," 3n8, 4
childlike jokes, in *SMiLE*, 3
childlikeness
  correlation between faith and, 22
  laughter and, 23
  philosophy of, 4
children
  bound up in the experience of other people, 116
  song of, 23–24, 93
"chill response," to music, 70
chord structure, of "Our Sweet Love," 122
Christ. *See also* Jesus
  believing in, 32
  cosmic, 129
  discerning, 138
  as incarnate within creativity, 136
  present in creative activities, 142
Christ In a Pluralistic Age (Cobb), 137
Christian, Roger, 96
A Christian Natural Theology (Cobb), 127
Christian theology, 26, 130
Christians, defining love for, 135
Chuck Berry, 80
"Chug-a-Lug," 78
Claremont School of Theology, 127
clinical depression, placebos treating, 76

Cobb, John B., Jr, 127, 128, 129
Coca-Cola cans, as musical instruments, 44
commandments of God, requirement of perfect submission to, 103
commitment, compared to possession, 121
"Commonwealth of God," 140–41
communal spirit, message of, 111
communication, establishing, 114
composition, Brian Wilson's modular approach to, 14
compositional complexity, arising from receptivity, 18
conformity, as enemy of self-trust, 44
connection
  emotional, between lyrics and listeners, 72
  between life of the mind and of the body, 114
  music as a possible agent for, 124
  between spirituality and childlike joy, 26
  vulnerability as the birthplace of, 101
conscious experience, 130
consciousness, in *Pet Sounds*, 36, 37
consistency, as enemy of self-trust, 44
contact, with others, 117
content, separating from form, 7
contradiction, in Beach Boys songs, 95–96
controlling consciousness, 36, 39
"Cool, Cool Water," 124
Corgan, Billy, 84n7
cosmic Christ, 129
cosmic Logos, identified with Christ, 138
cosmology, alternative, 128
Costello, Elvis, 107
courage, 55, 56
The Courage To Be (Tillich), 48
Couri, Al, 35
creation
  altering humankind's relationship to existence, 62
  answering existential questions, 64
  divine enjoyment of, 141
  lure of God active throughout, 134

Index

creative love, of God, 134, 135, 138
creative power, God's persuasive, 134
creative responsibility, Brian Wilson holding on to, 58
creative transformation, 129, 138–39, 142
creative transformaton, 136–37
creative-responsive love, 128, 138
creativity, cosmic vision of, 142

daily existence, anxiety of, 86
"Dance, Dance, Dance," 29, 80
death, Brian Wilsoln preoccupied with, 57
death knell, sounding, 45
death of God theologies, going against, 130
DeCurtis, Anthony, 6
dementia, music therapy for people with, 72–73
denial, 104
dependence, 19, 42
depression, treatment of, 70, 76
Descartes, 116, 131
Descartian dualistic notions, of pure spirit, 115
"Desolation Row" (Dylan), 28
despair
    creating melodies for moments of great, 40
    falling into, 38
    moving steadily into, 37
    Pet Sounds ending on a note of, 45
"destitute time," 53
Dickinson, Emily, 46
dire wave, 63–66
disclosure, of history rather than closure, 128
disclosures of Christ, art as, 136
divine "call," metaphor of, 133–34
divine commitment, to relationship (covenant), 85n10
divine empathy, 140
divine experience, 141
divine life, 141
divine lure, 133, 137
divine power, as persuasive, 127
divine radiance, 62, 65

divinity, trusting your, 16
"Do You Remember," 80
"Does it really matter?," 62
"Don't Back Down," 81, 101
"Don't Talk," 39–40
"Don't Worry Baby," 96–99
doors of perception, unlocking, 33
The Doors of Perception (Huxley), 16
dopamine, production of, 70
"doper song," 43
Dorrien, Gary, 127
dorsolateral prefrontal cortex, 19
"drive," as a push to directly enact the "loss," 89
drugged person, less responsive to others, 20
drugs. *See* mind-altering drugs
dualistic notions, of pure spirit as different from pure matter, 115
dualistic world view, with material and secular divided from spiritual and sacred, 136
Dumb Angel, 17
Dunbar, Reggie, 110
Dylan, Bob, 28

electronic culture, in the twenty-first century, 65–66
Elvis, 80
Emerson, Ralph Waldo, 27, 32, 33, 42, 46
emotional connection, between lyrics and listeners, 72
emotional contagion, 70–71, 78
emotions
    expressing through music, 70
    impacting our brains, 74
Endless Summer album, 83
endorphins, 75
endurance, of the abyss, 55
English horn, 40
enjoyment, that never comes, 88
enlightenment
    according to Kant, 12
    as a children's song, 24
    of seeing God, 93
epistemic dimension, of faith, 13–14
esthetic sphere, 87

Index

eternal objects, 132–33
"the ethereal tides," 33
ethical core, 87–88
Eve (Adam and), shame of exposure, 97
"Eve of Destruction" (McGuire), 28
events
    affecting God's own experience, 141
    notion of, 128
    saved and transformed into the divine life, 140
existential anxiety, facing, 62
existential securities, as gone, 53
experiences
    actual occasions of, 130
    communicating with other, 117n29
    some breaking the will, 63
extreme sports, worlds and languages of, 86

Fab Four. *See* Beatles
faith
    bound up with grace, 13
    character of, 18–19
    Christian, 20
    corresponding to and leading to joy, 22
    defined, 12, 18
    dimensions of, 13
    distinctive character of, 10–14
    freeing us to be children, 22
    lifting weight of worth of existence, 21
    Pinker's negative definition of, 12
    prone to misunderstanding, 10
    relationship with "reason," 11, 18
    relying on what is freely given, 13
    twofold character of, 11
    validating the self, 14
falling darkness, 52
false or illusory love, 124
feeling(s), 123–24, 130
fides quaerens intellectum (faith seeking understanding), 18
"fight or flight response," 74
finitude, 61, 122
fleeting moments, confidence in intrinsic value of, 140
flight, mental as well as physical, 104
Forde, Gerhard, 101
"Forever," 113, 121–22, 123
Four Freshmen, 77
"409," 409-cubic-inch (6.7 L) engine, 79
Freud, Sigmund, 103
fullness of being, 62
"Fun, Fun, Fun," 29, 80
future, open even for God, 127
future possibilities, 132

Garland, Judy, 104
generative dimension, of faith, 19
genius
    expected from Brian Wilson, 105
    most romantic type of, 98
    romanticized tragedy of, 49
gift from God, humor as, 22
glockenspiel, 41
God
    being with Brian Wilson, 3, 34
    of the Bible, as love, 134
    as both creative and responsive love, 135
    as both ground of infinite novelty and principle of limitation, 133
    creatively acting in the world, 135
    as "creative-responsive love," 128
    dipolar like all actualities, 135
    enfolding us, 141
    enjoying Beauty, 141
    as forever alive in, 141
    hearing, 23, 93
    as love, 127, 134
    messengers of, 101
    as nontemporal, 135
    not able to coerce, determine, or intervene in creation, 134
    not spatially limited, 135
    as the One Who Calls us, 133
    openness and receptivity to, 20
    as "poet of the world," 129
    prehending other actualities, 140
    presence of, 32, 99
    providing world with sense of order and novelty, 133
    uniquely present in Jesus, 138

Index

working patiently with every creaturely decision, 134
working under the form of opposites (*sub contrario*), 100
"God Only Knows," 33, 34, 41–43, 101, 104
gods, provided foundation, 53
Godself, 133
good times, 78, 80
"Good to My Baby," 104
"Good Vibrations," 16–17, 38, 77, 90
Gospel, 102
gospel of love, spreading through records, 7, 9, 124
grace
    appreciating the experience of, 102
    as the engine of the world, 26
    God of, blessing the undeserving, 99
    indicating God's free and open-handed goodness, 13
    iniating for every occasion, 134
    pointing the listener to source of, 60
    promise of, 13
    as unfair, 99
gratification, deficiency of, 88
gratitude, expressing without psychic protection, 104
greatest hits package, 29
greatness, misunderstanding of, 44
Groopman, Jerome, 67, 74
guidance, to make healing sounds, 2

"Hang on to Your Ego," 43, 44
happiness, 31
"happy glow," loss of, 45
harmonic and sonic palate, in "'Til I Die," 60
harmonic complexity, of "Good Vibrations," 17
harmonies
    personal problems counterbalanced vocal, 50
    representing moments of sheer transcendence, 77
    symbolizing unity, 78
harmony
    Beauty and, 139
    everlasting and growing, 140

"Harmony of Harmonies," 142
Hartshorne, Charles, 130
Hastings Center, 67
Hawthorne High School, 80
healthy-minded individual, 90
"healthy-minded soul," 90
heart-felt fantasy, bordering on prayer, 98–99
heart-on-your-sleeve auteur, 97
Heidegger, Martin, 47, 52, 61, 66
Heidelberg Disputation (Luther), 100
"Help Me, Rhonda," 29
helplessness, confession of, 59
Hendrix, 49
"Here Today," 42, 43, 140
"Heroes and Villains," 105, 107
hero's Homeric return from darkness, 51
Heschel, Abraham Joshua, 85
Highway 61 album (Dylan), 28
Hill, Joe, 72
hobby, addictive, 85–86
"holy song," singing, 56
hope
    altering pain processing, 76
    biology of, 74, 75
    in Christian theology, 68
    as counter to nonbeing, 55
    as life force of "Til I Die," 66
    philosophical importance of, 68
    playing a major role in healing, 67
    power of, 73–77
    promoting physical and psychological healing, 68
    songs as emblems of, 81
    unleashing a powerful emotion, 67
    using the same chemical pathways as analgesics, 76
hope-filled symbolism, 79
hopefulness, producing an atmosphere of, 66
"horizon of expectations," transformed by events, 128
"house of being," language as, 52
"How I Got Over" (Ward), 60n25
Hughes, Howard, 49
human beings

Index

experiencing the divine lure as a "call," 133
looking at from the outside, 116
problems in the twentieth century, 52
reflection on, 59
human condition, as unrooted, 47
human situation, expressing courageously, 64
humanity
  precarious position of, 117–18
  seeing the connectedness of all, 125
humor, 22
Huxley, Aldous, 16

"I Can Hear Music," 69
"I Get Around," 6, 29, 31, 80, 96, 104
"I Just Wasn't Made for These Times," 38, 41, 44, 89, 104
"I Know There's an Answer," 43, 44
"I wanna cry" lyrics, in "You Still Believe in Me," 39
illumination, production of, 54
illuminative beauty, of "'Til I Die," 62
"I'm Bugged at My Old Man," 100
"I'm Waiting for the Day," 38, 40
immaturity, according to Kant, 12
impossibility of *jouissance*, 88
"In My Room," 6, 36
individual thinking things, 117
injections, producing a stronger placebo effect than pills, 75
innate disposition, refusing negativity and unhappiness, 90
"inner" life, relating to other persons, 117
inner self, straightening out and unifying, 91
innocence, 3, 36, 45
instrumentals, in "This Whole World," 113–14
instruments, un-rock and roll, 37, 44
internalized influences, aesthetic synthesis of, 130
interventionist God, Cobb's argument against, 134
ironclad expectation, tending to stifle self-expression, 106

James, William, 90, 92
Janata, Petr, 72–73
Jardine, Alan, 30, 30n3, 41, 98, 122n40
jazz improvisation, 19
Jesus. *See also* Christ
  on being childlike, 22
  faithful responses to God's call, 138
  on innocence, 4
  not experiencing God as "other," 138
  "truly God and truly human," 138
  urging men and women to be children, 22
Johnston, Bruce, 42, 48
Jones, Brian, 49
Joplin, 49
joy, 21
joy and laughter, emphasis on, 10
"jubilate," Augustine's definition, 25
jubilation, 25
judgment, all fearing, 103
"junkie culture," 85

Kalinich, Steve, 110
Kant, on enlightenment, 19, 24
Kennedy, John F., 6, 89
kenotic love, 129
key changes, in "Our Sweet Love," 122
Kierkegaard
  on building up, 124–25
  championed the paradoxical, 92
  under the esthetic sky, 87–88
  on love, 5
  love as up-building, 113, 124–25
  security as religious stage or sphere of existence, 93
  seeking to diagnose the self, 92
knowledge, faith prerequisite for true, 18
"Kokomo," 83
Kreider, Tim, 101

Lambert, Philip, 22, 25, 41, 111
laughter, religious significance of, 23
the Law
  Brian Wilson struggling with, 103–4
  bringing wrath, 106
  commanding, 102

Index

the Law *(continued)*
    divine standard of righteousness, 102
    mandating love but not inspiring it, 105–6
    object lesson in the fruits of, 104
    thorny relationship with, 103
Law of *SMiLE*, 106
lead vocal, putting three- and four-part harmonies against, 78
Leaf, David, 34
Leary, Timothy, 16
Lennon, John, 45
"Let's Go Away for Awhile," 40–41, 104
Levitin, Daniel, 69
life
    coming and going of, 122
    meaningless without God's responsive love, 141
"Like a Rolling Stone" (Dylan), 28
Limb, Charles J., 19
"Little Deuce Coupe," 78, 79–80, 88
Little Richard, 80
Logos Christology, Cobb's cosmic, 137
"lost masterpiece," pop music's ultimate, 106–7
love. *See also* responsive love
    apocalypse of, 139
    awakening and hope born out of, 83
    bringing into "another day," 114
    as certain, 120
    course of moving downward, 43
    entangled with weakness, 102
    expressions of, 38
    as fundamental impulse of reality, 26
    of God, 101
    inner reality of, 5
    lasting forever, 122
    mattering to God, 140
    in the midst of weakness, 97
    as origin of everything, 125
    perishing, 140
    referencing specific instances of, 114
    "should" last forever, 123
    shown through musical and lyrical gifts, 113
    in spite of the uncertainty of the world, 120
    stretching our concept of, 122
    true nature of, 114
    understanding of God based on, 140
    as a way of perceiving the world, 111
Love, Mike, 2, 30, 34, 38, 39, 43, 79, 105, 110, 120, 125
love affair, beyond the finite, 123
love and innocence, perceiving and communicating, 3–4
"Love and Mercy," 102
"love and mercy," of God, 108–9
Love and Mercy: The Life, Love, and Genius of Brian Wilson (feature film), 49n3
love song, deceptively simple, 122
lover
    meeting the beloved at point of (persistent) failure and weakness, 102
    overcome with the reality of love, 123
loving someone, at their worst, 101
LSD. *See also* mind-altering drugs
    Brian Wilson experimenting with, 15
    Brian Wilson introduced to, 33
    Brian Wilson's deep regret at having used, 20
    opened Brian Wilson to voices, 20
    releasing the mind from control, 16
    trips, 33
    as ultimate joyride, 17
Luke 18:16–17, 4
lure
    divine, 133
    of God, 134, 138
Luther, Martin, 100, 102
lyrics
    differing dramatically from ordinary speech, 71
    emtional connection and, 72
    of *Pet Sounds*, 44, 127
    of *SMiLE* distinguished by wordplay, 107
    of "Surf's Up," 4, 23–24
    of "'Til I Die," 56

Mallarme, on distinctiveness of poetic language, 119

Index

Mama Cass, 49
Manson, Charles, 110
"A Many-Tiered Man" (poem), 103
Marcel, Gabriel, 7–8, 114, 117n29, 121–22
marijuana and hasish, for a creative and spiritual state of mind, 17
Marilyn
    "Caroline No" reflecting situation with, 45
    divorce in 1979, 42
Martin, George, 46
materialist outlook, 92
McCartney, Paul, 42–43, 46, 105
McGuire, Barry, 28
meaning, experiencing, 64
meaninglessness, torment of, 92
medial prefrontal cortex, 72–73
meeting of minds, 117–18
Menninger, Karl, 4n9
mental images, as "internal triggers" of emotions, 71
mental pole
    God's, 135
    prehending future possibilities, 132
Merleau-Ponty, Maurice, 111, 112, 115–16, 117n29
    certainty only with reservations, 120
    on feelings, 123–24
    on love and will, 123
    making reference to painting, 118
    on music, 118–19
mescaline, 16
mesolimbic system, undergoing stimulation, 70
metaphors for self, in "'Til I Die," 59
metaphysical reasons, for Cobb's total rejection of omnipotence, 134
micro-apocalypse, of love, 129, 142
Miłosz, Czesław, 103
mind
    with a body, 112
    revealing a struggling to stay afloat, 39
mind and body, not two substances, 131
mind or soul, as a series of occasions, 131
mind-altering drugs. *See also* LSD
    associated with spirituality, 15
    Brian Wilson and, 5, 78
    experience of taking, 20
    inhibiting receptivity, 20
    as a route to spirituality and religious experience, 16
    "Universal Being" sought through, 33
mistaken or illusory love, 124
modernity, 47, 52
"modular" approach
    "Good Vibrations" and, 17
    to recording, 14
Mojo, ranked *Pet Sounds* as the greatest album, 46n62
Moltmann, Jürgen, 21, 25, 134
Morrison, Jim, 49
mother, singing to her children, 24, 25, 26, 93, 108
"motherese," music evolved from, 69
Movement of Spiritual Inner Awareness, 2
music
    acoustic patterns in, 71
    as agent for change and connection, 124
    beginning of a new type of, 31
    continuing to inspire and restore, 81
    as deep, soul-satisfying medium, 120
    existing throughout human history, 69
    as an expression of spirit, 3
    as God's voice, 3, 9, 32, 96
    laden with truth, 7
    magic of, 69–73
    making of, healing Brian Wilson, 36
    new form of, 17
    penetrating the soul of the listener, 120
    raising levels of activity in the brain, 69–70
    reducing ability to perceive pain, 73
    reframing experience of, 128
    sending us back to, 8
    sounding whole, 32
    special content-form relation, 119
    as spiritual, 2, 7

Index

music *(continued)*
  stimulating emotions, 69
  stimulating memory, 73
music cognition, scientific study of, 69
musical daily lives, mundane occurrences of, 120
musical patterns, call-and-response, 135
musical structures and arrangements, of *Pet Sounds*, 37
musicosmology, 128, 142

nakedness, of Brian Wilson, 97
natural theology, remaining necessary, 130
natural world, reconnection to, 54–55
negative suggestions, affecting the body, 75
neoliberal capitalism, 87n18
Nietzsche, on threat of nihilism, 139
nihilism, threat of, 139
nocebo effect, 75
Nolan, Tom, 15
nonbeing
  acceptance of, 57
  coming to terms with, 61
  encounter with the threat of, 64
  as an ever-present component of being, 62
  as a part of one's own being, 55
  resolving Brian Wilson's questions, 62
nonconformity, world whipping with displeasure, 35
nonconscious experience, 130
"not enoughness," feelings of, 103
nothingness, creating something in the face of, 55
novel possibilities, God's provision of, 133

objective element, of faith, 11
"objective immortality," 131
objects
  difference between the loss of and loss, 88–89
  in dreams, 115

occasions
  actual, 130, 132
  capable of some degree of freedom, 131
  dipolar, 132
  initiating grace for, 134
ocean, surfer depending on, 85
ocean waves, rhythm of, 80
O'Hagan, Sean, 87
Ok Computer, 46
omnipotence, Cobb's total rejection of, 134
omni-potential God, versus onmi-potent, 134
"once-born," 90
Ono, Yoko, 45
ontological dimension, of faith, 13–14
ontology, Cobb rejecting both monism and dualism, 131–32
openness
  faith leading to, 14
  genuine, 20
optimism, compared to hope, 75
orchestrations, within structures, 37
"The Origin of the Work of Art" (Heidegger), 52n6
other
  starting from, 117n29
  transcending otherness, 114
other beings, knowing through their bodies, 115
"oughts," 103
Our Prayer, 3
"Our Sweet Love," 113, 122–25
outcome, God cannot determine any, 134
"oversouling," 43

pain
  placebos treating, 76
  from something deeper, 36
pain management, using music, 73
painting, 111, 112
"Pandora's Box," hope's role in the story of, 68
Parks, Van Dyke, 3, 6, 10, 17, 25, 87, 92, 107

Index

partnership, at the core of the Beatles, 105
Party! album, 29, 30
past, of the world, 130–31
past actualities, 132
past influences, final synthesis of, 131
Paul, (Apostle), on the Law, 102–3
perceiving, compared to defining, 118
perception
    immediacy of, 123
    unlocking doors of, 33
perpetual perishing, 129, 139, 141
personal experience, capturing the impact of, 59
perspectives, importance of, 115
Pet Sounds album, 89–90
    achievement of, 45–46
    apocalyptic character of, 128
    artistic impact of, 46
    Brian Wilson writing, 31
    cataloging ways we defend against nakedness, 104
    concept of, 36
    discerning Christ in, 138
    as an instance of Christ's creative immanence, 129
    as an instance of creative transformation, 138–39
    key changes, 122
    lyrical themes in, 129
    as most important album, 126–27
    not selling as well, 104
    as one of greatest albums of all time, 46
    perpetual perishing in, 139–43
    power and internal logic of, 36–37
    prayer sessions before recording, 2
    pre, 27–30
    pushed Beatles to reach high, 48
    quest for wholeness in, 27–46
    reaching the sublime with, 34, 37
    recording of, 99
    responsive love of God in, 139–42
    revolutionary album in the history of music, 127
    sessions as mystical, 33
    songs in, 1, 37–45
    struggle over the loss of youth, 139–40
    surpassing, 17
    wholeness of, 36–37
"Pet Sounds" song, 44
Peter, Saint, 102
Pets Sounds Revisited tribute album, 1
Phenomenology of Perception (Merleau-Ponty), 119
physical pole, 132, 135
physical world, immersion in, 84
Pieper, Josef, 14
Pinker, Steven, 11–12
placebo effect, studying, 74–76
pleasure centers, of the brain, 70
poet
    re-attaching things to nature and the Whole, 32
    in the time of the world's night, 61
poetic language, distinctiveness of, 119
poetry, 119
"poles," of every occasion, 132
pop structure, of songs, 37
possibilities, becoming actual, 132
power, as essential definition of deity, 134
prayers, Brian Wilson writing down on paper, 33
"prehension," 130
pretentiousness, of everything, 26, 92, 108
primordial nature, God's, 135
primordial rhythm, of moving water, 65
"prisoners of hope," transforming us into, 81
process metaphysics, basic claim of Cobb's, 130
"process of expression," bringing "meaning into being," 119
process philosophy, 129
process theology
    Cobb's Christian, 127
    inspiration for Christian, 129
    interpreting musical experiments and existential lyrics in *Pet Sounds*, 128
    understanding of divine love, 134

Index

programmatic music, as an exception, 118
progressions, going up toward God, 39
pro-labor songs, 72
protest songs, 71–72
Proust, 112, 119
The Psychedelic Experience (Leary), 16
psychedelic rock groups, of the '90s, 93n32
psychological mechanisms, enabling music to evoke emotions, 70–71
puppy love, "mundane" aspects of, 114
pure intellect, ideal of, 117
pure spirit, knowing only ourselves as, 115

radical contingency, inescapable sense of, 139
"The Rainbow" (Wordsworth), 4n9
realist commitment, to relational theism, 130
reason
    defined, 12
    faith and, 11
    standing before us, 117–18
receptivity
    cultivating, 26
    drugs inhibiting, 20
    faith leading to, 14
    of a person taking a drug, 16
    SMiLE and, 14–21
    transcendent experience and, 16
reclusiveness, of Brian Wilson, 49
record labels, albums and, 28
recording process, openness and contingency in, 15
reductionist materialisms, 131
relational image, of creation, 127
relational theism, encountering Cobb's, 132
relationship, reinvigorating a failing, 39
reliance, beyond self, 12
religion, essence of all, 2
religious aura, of the spirit of surfing, 86
religious experience, on LSD, 15
religious states, contrasting two, 90

repentance, created a boundless space, 93
"response beyond fate" principle, 57
responsive love, of God, 129, 135, 140, 141
resurrections, of the world into God, 141
Revolver album (Beatles), 105
Richards, Keith, 28
rock and roll, as a tough man's game, 97
rock and roll prayer, 121
rock and roll stardom, casualties of, 49
rock opera, to God, 10
Roholt, Tiger, 111–12
Rubber Soul album (Beatles), 28, 48
"Run James Run," 44

Sabbath, 85, 85n10
salvific divine reality, 140
Sapere aude! (Dare to be wise!), 12
"satisfaction," of the present occasion, 131
schizoaffective disorder, 49, 77
Schwartz, Loren, 33
Sea of Tunes Publishing, ownership of, 31
second birth, as a rediscovery, 94
Second Letter to the Corinthians, Apostle Paul's, 96
A Secular Age (Taylor), 84
secular time, 84, 86
self
    as focus of great art, 46
    as an instrument of language, 117
self-censorship, Brian Wilson's limited, 100
self-conscious selfhood, transcending, 16
self-destruction, of rock musicians, 50
self-incurred immaturity, 12
self-indulgence, symptoms of, 49
"Self-Reliance" (Emerson), 46n63
Sense and Non-Sense (Merleau-Ponty), 112–13
Sermon on the Mount, 102

Index

Sgt. Pepper's Lonely Hearts Club Band album (Beatles), 28, 46, 48, 105, 127
"She Knows Me Too Well," 102
shout, as a wordless sound of joy, 25
Shut Down Volume 2, 29
sick souls, 90–92
Siegel, Jules, 9, 23, 92
simplicity, beauty and sophistication of, 6
singing, double-tracked, 113
singles, all-important around 1964, 28
"Sloop John B.," 41, 104
SMiLE album, 9–10
   abandonment of, 5
   best songs outstripping *Sgt. Pepper's*, 107
   Brian Wilson's vision of, 17
   carrying painful associations, 106
   emerging from creative activity, 17
   "essence of all of religion," 2
   "faith-like" character of, 24
   joy and, 21–26
   musical aims of, 3
   receptivity and, 14–21
   recording and eventual shelving of, 104
   as shorthand for a different kind of Law, 106
   spiritual vision of, 25
   title as childlike, 5
The SMiLE Sessions, 15
Solidarity, 72
sonata, musical meaning of, 119
song
   of children, 25, 108
   of God, 24, 25
   of God's love, 26
song lyrics. *See* lyrics
sonic cathedrals, 66
"sophisticated-feeling music," 36
soul, connecting to the "Sunday mornin' Gospel," 119–20
space, viewed as a medium with a point of view, 112
sphere of fulfillment, as religious, 93
Spirit
   ground and foundation of the life of, 125
   presence of throughout creation, 133
   vessel for, 65
"spirit," of surfing, 86
spiritual language, Brian Wilson using, 99
spiritual music, according to Brian Wilson, 24
spiritual sound, creating, 10, 15
spiritual tune, "This Whole World" as, 113
spirituality
   of awakening and hope, 82–94
   Brian Wilson's quest for in *Pet Sounds*, 32–34
   independent of organized religion, 32
   like ever-lasting love, 101
   LSD and other mind-altering drugs associated with, 15
   openness and receptivity and, 19
Sprague, Ted, 2
stahlhartes Gehause (iron cage), 84
static permanence, things having, 131
Stendhal, notions of Ego and Liberty, 112
"still-to-be-determined" element, of modular composition, 15
Stohler, Christian, 76
straight male nerd's Judy Garland, 104
stroke patients, music therapy for, 72
struggle over the loss of youth, as a lyrical theme in *Pet Sounds*, 139–40
studio, like a church for Brian Wilson, 32
"subjective" element, of faith, 11
sublime release, laughter as, 22
substance and deliverance, experiencing lack of, 89
sugar pill, 75
Summer Days (and Summer Nights!!) album, 29, 100

Index

Sunflower album, perceiving and building up love in, 110–25
"superego," 103
surf culture
    celebrating and enabling a "junkie culture," 85
    coincidence with rise in popularity of, 83
    desire for image of the chill surfer, 88
    inviting people not to worry about tomorrow, 87
    nature of, 84
    thin in terms of historical content, 86
    as very territorial and hierarchical, 84–85
surf groups, ritualized spirituality, 86n14
surfer gangs, emergence of, 84
"Surfer Girl," 78
surfers, chasing the ecstatic, 85
"Surfin' Safari," 78, 79
"Surfin' U.S.A.," 78, 79
surfing
    activity of, 84–85
    cannot save human beings, 88
    embodying hope, 78–79
    experienced as Sabbath, 85
    as much more than a hobby, 86
    requires waiting and patience, 85
    at risk of becoming like a drug, 86
    risking reduction to a religious commodity, 87
    wanting the high of the wave, 88
surfing, beach, and summer fun themes, transcended in "Surf's Up," 83
surfing songs, as a kind of American mythology, 87
surfing time, as Sabbath, 84–88
"Surf's Up," 92, 107
    about an awakening to joy and hope, 93
    Brian Wilson and, 108
    composition of, 92
    double entendre of the title, 83
    exegesis of, 23
    lyrics of, 4
    mature voice of newfound hope, 82–83
    musical exposition of, 24
    security not found in the usual places, 93
    as "the soul of *Smile*," 25
    vocal arrangement in, 4–5
Surf's Up album, "'Til I Die" released on, 47, 57
"Sweet Little Sixteen" (Berry), 79
symphony, with God, 65
"symphony to God." *See also* teenage symphony
    SMiLE as, 108

Taylor, Charles, 84
tears, teenage male, 97
"technological day," 54, 66
teenage symphony. *See also* "symphony to God"
    to God, 3, 10, 17, 56, 104
tempo, 24
Ten Commandments, 85, 102
terror, 53
"test song," 30n3
"That's Not Me," 39, 41
themes, of faith, hope, and love, 6
theo-cosmology, Cobb's, 128, 129–36
theology, Christian, 26, 130
Theology and Joy (Moltmann), 21
Theology of Culture (Tillich), 48
"theology of glory," 100–101
"theology of the cross" (*theologia crucis*), 100
therapeutic tool, music as, 72
This is Your Brain on Music: The Science of a Human Obsession (Levitin), 69
"This Whole World," 111, 113–19
thought and body, bound up together, 116
Thunderbird sports car, 80
"Ticket to Ride" (Beatles), 29
"'Til I Die," 56–59
    attitude of, 62
    composed in Brian Wilson's dark time, 48
    as a conversation, 65

Index

dark energy behind, 53
intended for an earlier post-*Pet Sounds* album, 57
loosening grip of finitude and non-being, 57
modeling a place to stand, 63
modeling the courage to be, 56
not a witness of Brian Wilson's pain and suffering, 58–59
nuanced with wisdom, 63
questions in, 52, 59–63
reasons for writing, 61
unanswered theological questions, 66
Tillich, Paul, 48
courage as best posture, 61
on grappling with questions of being, 64
prescribed courage in the face of the abyss, 55
prescription for spiritual and psychological well-being, 57
sense of the times, 52
time and history, real for God, 135
"The Times They Are A-Changin'," 30
timpani blasts, reflecting "a throbbing, aching heart," 40
Today!, 29
Tomaino, Concetta, 73
"Tomorrow Never Knows" (Beatles), 16
transcendence, 114
transience, 93, 139
trust, 12, 21
truth of being, revealing, 54
Turn! Turn! Turn! album (Byrds), 28
"turning," facilitating humankind's, 54
Tutu, Desmond, 81n47
twice-born, religion of, 90–91

ukulele, adding neat fills, 40
uncertainty, estimated as certainty, 120
unchildish childhood question, faith answering, 21
underground cultures, romanticized, 86
unhappiness, characterizing order-making and struggle, 91

unique actuality, 132, 133
Universal Being, 32, 33
University of Wisconsin, fight song, 80
unpredictableness, of Brian Wilson's creativity, 35
unrequited love, emotional instability and confusion of, 40
"until I die," as the answer, 60
up-building, desire for, 124

valid artists, 54, 55, 56
Varieties of Religious Experience (James), 90
venturing out, 18, 19
victimhood, identity and experience of, 92
visual imagery, 71
vocal harmonies, 77
voices, opened to Brian Wilson by LSD, 20
Vosse, Michael, 23
vulnerability, 100, 101

"Wake the World," 73
Ward, Clara, 60n25
"Warmth of the Sun," 6, 89
wave
riding, 63
searching for the perfect, 67–81
weakness, as strength, 98
weakness and shame, knowing someone fully in, 102
weaknesses, delighting in, 96
Wexler, Jerry, 43
"What Are Poets For?" (Heidegger), 47, 52, 54, 65
"What is Enlightenment?" (Kant), 12, 22
"When I Grow Up (To Be a Man)," 29
White, Timothy, 44
Whitehead, Alfred North, 129
on eternal objects, 132
on incarnation of God in the world, 133
philosophy of, 130
view of God, 140
Whitman, Walt, 46

165

Index

wholeness
  Brian Wilson achieved, 37
  insistence on, 32
  possibility of, 56
The Will to Believe (James), 92
willingness, to be seen as weak, 101
Wilson, Brian
  abused as a child, 6
  activity prior to release of *Sunflower*, 110
  ambition to redraw the entire map of pop music, 30
  anticipated conflicts, 44
  anxiety breakdown, 27–28
  art outsized his learning and taste, 99
  challenging Beatles' creative supremacy, 48
  Christian tradition shaping early life, 1–2
  competing with the Beatles, 89
  consciousness of, 36
  creating daring, and profound music, 27
  as a creative force, 50, 77
  deaf in his right ear, 77
  drug use and psychological issues, 5
  emerging self, 30–31
  family members rejecting his work, 105
  feeling competition with the Beatles, 105
  fired his father as manager, 31
  floodgate, opening an emotional, 97
  on "Forever," 121
  genius of, 98, 105
  hearing voices, 77
  illegal drugs and, 78
  interest in religion, 2
  internalizing success of *Sgt. Pepper* as anticipated condemnation, 105
  interpretation of lyrics of "Surf's Up," 4
  isolation, obsession with, 83
  as lyricist for "Caroline, No," 140
  marriage to Marilyn, 42
  mature music as evidence of a broken but healing artist, 92
  mental illness of, 77
  modular approach to recording, 14
  music-making expressed in spiritual terms, 96
  myth of, 49
  not celebrating success of *Party!*, 30
  notoriety of, 49
  performed most lead vocals on *Pet Sounds*, 34
  prayers of, 2–3, 33
  ran out of interest in surfing, 88
  refusing to veil his neediness, 97
  remarks about "Surf's Up," 92–93
  resurrected *SMiLE* sans Boys, 107
  retirement from touring, 48–49
  retreated to his room for fifteen years, 106
  reverence for, 1
  search for a spiritual sound, 10
  speaking of songs in spiritual terms, 124
  on spiritual sound, 9
  struggling with the Law, 103–4
  "This Whole World," 113
  unique sound created by, 84n7
  wholeness achieved by, 37
  wrote both lyrics and music of "'Til I Die," 56
Wilson, Carl, 2, 41, 42, 43, 57, 65, 110, 120, 125
  as co-writer of "Our Sweet Love," 122n40
  praying for light and guidance, 33
  on spiritual side of music, 3
Wilson, Dennis, 6, 30, 78, 110, 125
  singing "Forever," 121
  surfed, 83
Wilson, Murry, 2, 31, 110
Wiman, Christian, 86
"Wonderful," 4
word, of God as a children's song, 108
Wordsworth, William, 4n9
world, reacting upon God, 135
A World of Peace Must Come album, 110
The World of Perception (Merleau-Ponty), 118
world's night, 47, 52

166

Index

"Wouldn't It Be Nice," 37–38, 89, 104
wounded hero (genius), romanticized tragedy of, 49
Wrecking Crew, recording backing tracks for *Pet Sounds*, 34

Yorke, Thom, 46
"You Still Believe in Me," 38–39, 102
"Your Brain on Jazz," 19
"Your Summer Dream," 80
"You're under arrest" joke, in "Heroes and Villains," 3
youthful love, excitement of, 38
"You've Got to Hide Your Love Away," 29–30

Zahl, Paul, 103
Žižek, Slavoj, 88–89

www.ingramcontent.com/pod-product-compliance
Lightning Source LLC
Chambersburg PA
CBHW030113170426
43198CB00009B/610